Basic College Vocabulary Strategies

Third Edition

Darlene Canestrale Pabis

Westmoreland County Community College

Arden B. Hamer

Indiana University of Pennsylvania

PEARSON

Boston   Columbus   Indianapolis   New York   San Francisco   Upper Saddle River
Amsterdam   Cape Town   Dubai   London   Madrid   Milan   Munich   Paris   Montreal   Toronto
Delhi   Mexico City   São Paulo   Sydney   Hong Kong   Seoul   Singapore   Taipei   Tokyo

To Dale.—ABH

To my students, children and parents—thank you for your support.—DCP

Senior Acquisitions Editor: Nancy Blaine
Development Editor: Jamie Fortner
Marketing Manager: Kurt Massey
Senior Supplements Editor: Donna Campion
Executive Media Producer: Stefanie Snajder
Digital Project Manager: Janell Lantana
Production/Project Manager: Clara Bartunek
Project Coordination, Text Design, and Electronic Page Makeup: Nitin Agarwal/Aptara®, Inc.
Creative Director: Jayne Conte
Cover Designer: Suzanne Behnke
Cover Art: rudall30/Shutterstock
Printer/Binder: RR Donnelley
Cover Printer: RR Donnelley

This title is restricted to sales and distribution in North America only.

Credits and acknowledgments borrowed from other sources and reproduced, with permission, in this textbook appear on the appropriate page within text.

Library of Congress Cataloging-in-Publication Data

Pabis, Darlene Canestrale.
    Basic college vocabulary strategies / Darlene Canestrale Pabis, Arden
B. Hamer.—3rd ed.
        p. cm.
    Includes bibliographical references and index.
    ISBN-13: 978-0-321-83893-3 (alk. paper)
    ISBN-10: 0-321-83893-9 (alk. paper)
    1. Vocabulary—Problems, exercises, etc.   2. Learning and
scholarship—Terminology--Problems, exercises, etc. 3. Universities and
colleges—Curricula—Terminology—Problems, exercises, etc.   I. Hamer,
Arden B.   II. Title.
    PE1449.P24 2014
    428.1—dc23
                                                2012033567

9 17

ISBN 13: 978-0-321-83893-3
ISBN 10:   0-321-83893-9

A list of the pronunciation symbols used in this text is given below in the column headed AHD. The column headed Examples contains words chosen to illustrate how the AHD symbols are pronounced. The letters that correspond in sound to the AHD symbols are shown in boldface. Although similar, the AHD and IPA (International Phonetic Alphabet) symbols are not precisely the same because they were conceived for different purposes.

Examples	AHD	Examples	AHD
p**a**t	ă	b**oo**t	o͞o
p**ay**	ā	**ou**t	ou
c**are**	âr	**p**o**p**	p
f**a**ther	ä	**r**oa**r**	r
bi**b**	b	**s**auce	s
chur**ch**	ch	**sh**ip, di**sh**	sh
dee**d**, mill**ed**	d	**t**ight, stopp**ed**	t
p**e**t	ĕ	**th**in	th
b**ee**	ē	**th**is	*th*
fi**fe**, **ph**ase, rou**gh**	f	**c**ut	ŭ
ga**g**	g	**ur**ge, t**er**m, f**ir**m, w**or**d, h**ear**d	ûr
hat	h	**v**al**ve**	v
which	hw	**w**ith	w
p**i**t	ĭ	**y**es	y
p**ie**, b**y**	ī	**z**ebra, **x**ylem	z
p**ier**	îr	vi**s**ion, plea**s**ure, gara**ge**	zh
ju**dge**	j	**a**bout, it**e**m, ed**i**ble, gall**o**p, circ**u**s	ə
kick, **c**at, pi**que**	k	butt**er**	ər
lid, need**le**[1]	l (nēd′l)		
mu**m**	m		
no, sudde**n**[1]	n (sŭd′n)		
thi**ng**	ng		
p**o**t	ŏ		
t**oe**	ō		
c**au**ght, p**aw**, f**or**, h**o**rrid, h**oa**rse[2]	ô		
n**oi**se	oi		
t**oo**k	o͝o		

[1]In English the consonants *l* and *n* often constitute complete syllables by themselves.

[2]Regional pronunciations of -or- vary. In pairs such as **for, four; horse, hoarse;** and **morning, mourning,** the vowel varies between (ô) and (ō). In this Dictionary these vowels are represented as follows: **for** (fôr), **four** (fôr, fōr); **horse** (hôrs), **hoarse** (hôrs, hōrs); and **morning** (môr′ning), **mourning** (môr′ning, mōr′-). Other words for which both forms are shown include **more, glory,** and **borne.** A similar variant occurs in words such as **coral, forest,** and **horrid,** where the pronunciation of *o* before *r* varies between (ô) and (ŏ). In these words the (ôr) pronunciation is given first: **forest** (fôr′ist, fŏr-).

Why Do You Need This New Edition?

If you're wondering why you should buy the third edition of *Basic College Vocabulary Strategies*, here are six good reasons!

1. Chapter Objectives have been identified to help you focus on key skills.

2. A focus on how learning happens and the importance of using a variety of learning strategies.

3. Restructured outline so the Multiple Choice questions are now the first exercise you will complete to help the transition from a basic knowledge level to higher level thinking in the exercises that follow.

4. A new Appendix that offers the answers to the multiple choice feature will help you monitor your progress and focus your attention on problematic areas.

5. Updated Dictionary feature including the addition of the etymology and antonyms for each word!

6. New Vocabulary Words that provide a clearer understanding of the structural elements.

Contents

vi   Contents

Preface

Introduction and Purpose

An extensive vocabulary and the ability to decode unknown words are important for reading comprehension. We have designed this text to help college students attain both. Students will work directly with 153 words presented in the chapters. While learning the words, students will work with structural elements that will enable them to decode additional words. In addition to presenting vocabulary words, this text addresses vocabulary learning through memory and learning strategies. We hope that students will use these strategies to enhance their vocabulary learning and then transfer them to their learning in other courses.

Special Features

As mentioned, one important feature of this text is the emphasis placed on students' word attack skills for future reading and learning. Therefore, the words are grouped by structural elements, and information is given to help students use word attack skills and strategies to unlock future unknown words.

When effective readers encounter new words, they use several strategies to decode the word without interrupting their reading. The words in the chapters are presented in that format. First the words are presented with their pronunciations (See and Say) because students' listening vocabulary is often more extensive than their reading vocabulary. Second, structural elements are identified and defined. Next, the words are used in sentences with clear context clues, which mirror how content-specific words are presented in textbooks. Finally, the dictionary definition is given along with other information about the word to help the student have a deeper understanding of the meaning and usage of the word. This strategy (SSCD: See and Say, Structural Elements, Context Clues, Dictionary) is explained to the student in Chapter One.

The text also addresses students' vocabulary learning strategies. Chapter One includes information about learning in general and vocabulary in particular. This information about learning is reinforced throughout the chapters with Memory Tips and Vocabulary Strategies that can also transfer to the students' other classes. In Chapter One there are individual, small group, and whole class activities that the instructor can use in class, or assign as an out-of-class activity to help students understand their own learning and what they can do to make the most of their efforts. This information is presented in Chapter One as opposed to an Introduction because we want to emphasize the importance of students becoming independent in their word attack skills, vocabulary learning, and other learning situations.

New to This Edition

The third edition of *Basic College Vocabulary Skills* has many new features while keeping the same format that reviewers and users of the first and second editions have reported as beneficial for their students.

- A focus on how learning happens and the importance of using a variety of learning strategies.

- The Multiple Choice questions are now the first exercise students complete and the answers are included in the back of the book. This is in response to suggestions by the reviewers as well as students using the text. This also reinforces the flow from a basic knowledge level to higher level thinking in the exercises that follow.

- In the Dictionary section there are several additions:
  - The etymology of each word is given in order to further encourage knowledge and use of structural elements.
  - Antonyms are given for the words in addition to synonyms. This further expands the students' knowledge of the word as well as their vocabulary.

- There are several changes in the words selected for each chapter. These changes were made to reflect a clearer understanding of the structural elements.

There are also several additions to the Instructor's Manual:

* Five-minute Quick Teach ideas that can be used at the end of a class if there is extra time

* Pretests instructors can use to direct students' learning and motivation to learn

* PowerPoints that are available on the Pearson website

* For some chapters there are web addresses where the students can find videos to reinforce either their word knowledge or their understanding of the learning strategies.

Chapter Organization

There are nine chapters, each with two parts, A and B. In each part there are seven to nine words presented. This is the optimal number for learning; any more per section would be too much for students to master. At the end of each chapter there are two or three Power Words with one set of exercises. These words do not fit the structural elements, but are either interesting or important words for students to know.

The outline for each chapter is:

1. Motivational quotation

2. Memory Tip

3. Vocabulary Strategy

4. Part A and Part B that each contain:
   a. Words to learn with pronunciations
   b. Structural elements with definitions
   c. Words presented in context with context clues emphasized
   d. Dictionary information including etymology, meaning, another sentence, synonyms, and antonyms
   e. Practice Exercises:
      i. Multiple Choice
      ii. Fill in the Blank
      iii. Correct or Incorrect?
      iv. Short Answer

5. Power Words

6. Chapter Review
   a. Yes/No? or Matching exercise
   b. Expanded Word Forms
   c. Expand Your Learning
   d. Puzzle Fun

To the Instructor

We hope that you will find this text enjoyable to use as well as significant to your students' learning and success. With nine chapters, each with two parts and additional exercises, we are hopeful that you will be able to complete the entire book in one semester with your students. Please see the Instructor's Manual online for some ideas for classroom instruction.

To the Student

We enjoy words and language and hope that this is evident throughout the book. We also hope that you will "catch" some of this enjoyment and interest. We both have used this text in our classes with hundreds of students and have incorporated their input in this and previous editions. In addition to an interest in language, we also hope that you will "catch" our joy of learning. There is information in this book about how you can be most effective in learning new vocabulary. This information can be transferred to any new learning task, whether it is in a college course or on your job.

Acknowledgments

We are grateful to Eric Stano for his support of this third edition and to Nancy Blaine and Jamie Fortner for their continued help. We also want to acknowledge our early connections with Pearson/Prentice Hall and thank Ray Mesing and Craig Campanella. We are honored that several instructors who have used the second edition in their classrooms were willing to take the time to give detailed and useful feedback. Their feedback and ideas were great and we have incorporated many of them in this third edition. The reviewers were Diana Ferrell, Imperial Valley College; Laura Gritman, Tallahassee Community College; Dr. Elizabeth Price, Ranger College; and Adalia Reyna, South Texas College—Pecan. Our colleagues at Indiana University of Pennsylvania and Westmoreland County Community College always offer support. Finally, we are grateful to our families for their support, encouragement, and understanding of our obsession with this project.

CHAPTER ONE

Where Do I Begin?

*One forgets words as one forgets names.
One's vocabulary needs constant fertilizing or it will die.*

Evelyn Waugh, English novelist (1903–1966)

CHAPTER OUTLINE

How We Learn

Seven Steps to Memory

SSCD: A Vocabulary Strategy

Strategies for Learning Vocabulary

Format of Chapters and Important Terms

How We Learn

Before you start working in the chapters and adding to your vocabulary, it is important to understand how you learn so that your vocabulary learning is efficient and effective. Here is a definition:

Learning requires **varied** and **repeated** study spaced out **over time**.

The important words are *varied*, *repeated*, and *over time*! Here is what they mean:

Varied—In order to learn you need to work with the material in many different ways. Think about how you can use vision (color, pictures), sound, and touch (writing) when you are studying.

Repeated—Learning does not happen in one study session; it requires many study sessions.

Over time—These multiple and varied study sessions need to be spread out; you need time to absorb the information and get it securely into your memory.

Let's think about this before we move on specifically to vocabulary. Try one or more of these excercises. Your instructor may assign specific ones to the class.

1. (Individual exercise) As you go through your day, keep a list of all the activities you do using the material you are learning for your classes, either in class or during your study time. Then:
   a. At the end of the day analyze these activities using the bulleted points listed on the next page. What involved color, voices, charts, writing, etc.?
   b. Next, look through the Chapter Review sections in this text at the various ways to Expand Your Learning. What activities can you add to your studying to help you learn better?
   c. Be prepared to share your thoughts with your class at the next meeting.

2. (Individual and small group exercise) Think about your hardest subject and list what you normally do to learn the information. How many different strategies do you usually use? When do you begin studying?

Now get into a group of two or more. Share your answers and listen to what the others are doing. What strategies are they using that you can add to your studying? What strategies can you suggest to others that they might try?

3. (Small group and whole class exercise) Break into small groups. Each group chooses one subject that students in your institution commonly take and brainstorms how many different things you can do with the information to learn it. Consider strategies that use the different senses listed under the term *varied* used previously and the more specific strategies that follow. Share with whole class.

Here are some specific suggestions for using one or more senses to make your learning more meaningful and your efforts more efficient.

Using your vision and color:

- Think in pictures.

- Use color. For example, write with different-color pens, highlight, use different-color papers.

- Make charts, graphs, concept maps.

- Make concept cards with written information and a trigger word(s).

- Read other material and watch for vocabulary words and structural elements.

Using your voice and hearing:

- Explain the information to others.

- Repeat the information out loud.

- Listen to tapes of recorded information.

- Listen to and be aware of vocabulary words and structural parts used in conversation, on TV, in movies.

Using large and small muscles:

- Write and rewrite.

- Manipulate the information by making charts, graphs, diagrams, etc.

- Make concept cards that you handle while you study.

- Role-play.

Seven Steps to Memory

Here is some more information about learning and memory. The following seven steps will help you learn new vocabulary as well as anything else you want or need to learn. The preceding definition of learning fits into these seven steps. These steps will be further explained in Chapters Two through Eight.

1. *Intend to remember*—Sometimes this basic concept can be the difference between remembering and forgetting.

2. *Organize the material to be learned*—It is easier to learn and remember information that is organized in a meaningful way.

3. *Test/retest*—Restating information in your own words from memory will help the memorization process.

4. *Overlearn the material*—Making the information as readily available as possible is the goal, and that's what overlearning will do.

5. *Use memory techniques*—Being actively involved with the material, for example using visualization, association and mnemonics, promotes learning/remembering.

6. *Space your learning over several study sessions*—The capacity of memory dictates the need for several study sessions.

7. *Study before bed*—Review before bed to minimize the effects of interference.

SSCD: A Vocabulary Strategy

When you were in high school or even in elementary school your teachers told you that if you didn't know the meaning of a word you were to "look it up in the dictionary." Although that was sound advice at the time, it may not be as efficient now that you are in college.

You will be reading more textbooks in one semester than you did in an entire year of high school or middle school. The words you will encounter will be more challenging. Therefore, you should have a strategy to help you to unlock the meaning of unfamiliar words. One such strategy is **SSCD.** The primary advantage of SSCD is that you have tools to figure out the meaning of words and continue reading. Use the following explanation and steps to unlock new words, and remember to continue reading as soon as you know the meaning.

See and Say the Word: Try to pronounce the word. Your listening vocabulary is bigger than your reading vocabulary, so you may already know the word.

Structure: Use what you know about word parts to start to figure out the word.

Context Clues: Often the author will give you the definition of the word in the same sentence or surrounding sentences.

Dictionary: If all else fails, look up the word in the glossary of the textbook or a dictionary.

For example, consider the sentence:

George Washington never wrote an autobiographical account of his life, but many others wrote his biography.

You might be able to **say** the word *autobiographical*. Next, look at the structure of the word. Does the word have a prefix? Does it have a common word element that you know? For example, *auto-* , self; *bio-* , life; *-graph*, something written; *-al*, relating to.

Then use the **context clues** around the unfamiliar word *autobiographical*. What words helped you to determine the meaning of the word *autobiographical*?

You should have said, *never wrote... account of his life.* By using context clues, you will save countless hours, because you will not have to use the dictionary for word meaning. Besides the amount of time that you save, you will also improve comprehension because you will not have to leave the textbook material to look up a word and then come back to the text to understand the passage.

Sometimes the author will not give you context clues or you will not know the structural elements. At that point the only way to determine meaning is to look up the word. It is wise to use the glossary to begin your search for the meaning of the unfamiliar word, because the glossary provides discipline-specific word meanings.

These steps will be further explained in Chapters Two through Five.

Strategies for Learning Vocabulary

The preceding two sections offered information you can use when learning anything—information from your other classes, a new procedure on your job, names of people in a new group you have joined, etc. Here are some strategies specifically geared to learning vocabulary and working with the chapters in this book:

- Take your time and work through the SSCD sections. Try to develop your own definition before reading the one from the dictionary.

- Say the words out loud.

- Do the exercises in at least two different study sessions.

- Check your answers to the multiple choice questions in Appendix A to be sure you understand the words before moving on.

- Try to use the words in new sentences of your own.

- Every once in awhile, go back and review the chapters you previously did.

Format of Chapters and Important Terms

Each chapter follows the same format:

- Each chapter has a Part A and Part B with seven to nine words in each. The words are grouped according to common structural elements.

- The word definitions are presented following the SSCD format.

- Four practice exercises are given for each group of words, going from easy, literal practice to higher level thinking exercises.

- Power Words—These are interesting words you should know that don't fit into the structural elements.

- Each chapter ends with Chapter Review and Expand Your Learning exercises to help you review all of the words in the chapter using different learning strategies.

- Each chapter ends with Puzzle Fun so that you can have fun thinking about the words.

There is additional information in the dictionary section for each vocabulary word that will help you understand that word and also increase your vocabulary in general.

- Etymology—This is the definition of the word through the meaning of its structural elements.

- Synonyms—These are words that mean the same thing as the vocabulary word.

- Antonyms—These are words that mean the opposite of the vocabulary word.

One final thought:

As you begin your study, remember to enjoy language and learning.

CHAPTER TWO

Using Strategies to Learn New Words

The difference between the right word and the almost right word is the difference between lightning and lightning bug.

Mark Twain (1835–1910)

CHAPTER OBJECTIVE

Students will be able to identify and use words with the following common structural elements:

Prefixes: trans-, anti-, pre-, post-

CHAPTER OUTLINE

 Memory Tip   Intend to Remember

 Vocabulary Strategy   See and Say the Word

Part A
Words to Learn

transition	antisocial
transmit	antiestablishment
transport	antiseptic
transfer	antidote

Structural Elements

trans-

anti-

Part B
Words to Learn

preface	postpone
prefix	postscript
precede	
preview	
predict	

Structural Elements

pre-   post-

Power Words

affiliation	excerpt
inference	

Memory Tip   Intend to Remember

In Chapter One you read about seven steps that will help you remember and learn. The first is simple—Intend to Remember. When you are working on these vocabulary words or anything you are learning, have the intention of remembering and learning. Although it seems simple, this desire and intention to learn is the first step.

 ### *Vocabulary Strategy*   See and Say the Word

Our listening vocabulary is larger than our reading vocabulary. When you encounter a word you do not know in your reading, there is a chance you have heard the word and are familiar with it. The first step in learning a word is to see whether you can pronounce it. Maybe you have heard it before and have some idea of its mearning. In the section *Words to Learn—See and Say*, the pronunciation for each word is given. That is your first step!

Part A

 WORDS TO LEARN—SEE AND SAY   Use the pronunciation guide on the first page of this book to help you SAY each word.

1. transition   trăn-zĭsh′ən
2. transport   trăns-pôrt′
3. transmit   trăns-mĭt′
4. transfer   trăns-fûr′
5. antisocial   ăn′tē-sō′shəl
6. antiestablishment   ăn′tē-ĭ-stăb′lĭsh-mənt
7. antiseptic   ăn′tĭ-sĕp′tĭk
8. antidote   ăn′tĭ-dōt′

 STRUCTURAL ELEMENTS   Look at the structural elements of each word. Use these elements to unlock the word's meaning.

trans-   across, change
anti-   opposite, against

 CONTEXT CLUES   Read the sentences. Use the words around the unfamiliar word to determine the word's meaning. Words in bold are the vocabulary words; words in italic are the context clues.

1. It is difficult to **transition** *from being a carefree high school student to being an independent college student*.

2. When it comes time to **transport** the contents of the Smith mansion, it will be necessary to hire a professional *moving company*.

3. I cannot believe that a small light could **transmit** such illumination. The light that it *gave off* was enough for me to read my book.

4. *After completing* my first two years at Penn State University, I will **transfer** *to UCLA to complete* my degree in drama.

5. Sarah's **antisocial** *behavior* made it *difficult for her to work with other people* on group projects.

6. John was very **antiestablishment**; he *did not like anything the organization did* or how it went about doing it.

7. The doctor prescribed **antiseptic** ointment to *prevent my cut from getting infected*.

8. The **antidote**, or *remedy*, for the poison was only available at the Poison Control Center.

DICTIONARY   Read the following definitions.

1. **transition**   trăn-zĭsh′ən   noun

   Etymology: trans (across, change) tion (act, state, or condition of)

   Cross from one form, state, style, or place to another

   The **transition** between high school and college can be very difficult because *the change* involves living with someone other than your family.

   Synonyms: conversion, change, alteration

   Antonym: stagnation

2. **transport**   trăns-pôrt′   verb

   Etymology: trans (across, change) port (carry)

   To carry from one place to another; to carry across

   Jen and Dave had to rent a U-Haul to **transport** their furniture *from their old apartment to their new home.*

   Synonyms: carry, convey

   Antonym: keep

3. **transmit**   trăns-mĭt′   verb

   Etymology: trans (across, change) mit (send)

   To send from one person, thing, or place to another

   My professor said he would **transmit** my grades *electronically* because I won't be getting my grades in the mail.

   Synonyms: broadcast, dispatch

   Antonym: receive

4. **transfer**   trăns-fûr′   verb/noun

   Etymology: trans (across, change) fer (yield or bear)

   (verb) To move oneself from one location or job to another; to yield across

   Since the company bought a new warehouse on the other side of town, many of its employees have had to **transfer** *from one bus to another* at the main depot to get to work.

   (noun) A ticket or something that permits someone to go from one place to another

   It is more economical to buy a bus **transfer,** *or pass,* if you are going to travel by bus frequently.

   Synonyms: (verb) relocate, carry   (noun) ticket

5. **antisocial**   ăn′tē-sō′shəl   adjective

   Etymology: anti (opposite, against) social (relating to people and friendliness)

   Disruptive of the established social order and marked by or engaging in behavior that violates accepted social order

   One of the major complaints of Brandon's employer was his **antisocial** behavior that caused many of his coworkers to file complaints about his *disruptive attitude* in the workplace.

   Synonym: unfriendly

   Antonym: friendly

   Vocabulary Tip: To be *antisocial* implies being disruptive whereas being *unsociable* implies that one is not comfortable in a social situation.

6. **antiestablishment** ăn′tē-ĭ-stăb′lĭsh-mənt   adjective

   Etymology: anti (opposite or against) establishment

   Marked by opposition or hostility to conventional social, political, or economic values or principles; opposed to the established hierarchy, system, or leadership of a large government, corporation, church, or the like

   Be careful when listening to campaign promises of **antiestablishment** candidates because they will make promises that *go against the government* just to get elected.

7. **antiseptic** ăn′tĭ-sĕp′tĭk   adjective/noun

   Etymology: anti (opposite or against) septic (of unclean unknown origins)

   (adjective) Capable of preventing infection

   The **antiseptic** ointment proved to be effective *in clearing up the rash* that the baby had.

   (noun) Something capable of preventing infection

   The **antiseptic** that the doctor prescribed helped the young child *clear up his rash.*

   Synonyms: (adj) antibacterial, sterile

   Antonyms: unclean, contaminated

8. **antidote** ăn′tĭ-dōt′   noun

   Etymology: anti (opposite or against) dote (from the root *didonai*, which means "to give")

   A remedy for the effects of a toxin or poison

   The doctor was very clear when he told the child's mother that it was critical that her son get the **antidote** *for the snake bite* that he got while camping with the scouts.

   Synonyms: medicine, remedy

Practice Exercises

MULTIPLE CHOICE

1. Which of the following phrases would indicate a <u>transition</u> in a story?
   a. "The next thing that happened was . . ."
   b. "Beth ran out of the house."
   c. "When does school begin?"
   d. "I do not understand the French language."

2. How can you <u>transport</u> groceries?
   a. steaming or boiling
   b. canning
   c. in plastic bags
   d. with salt and butter

3. Why would you <u>transmit</u> messages?
   a. so someone far away could get them
   b. so they are written more clearly
   c. to make it easier to go from one class to another
   d. to be sure all your credits count toward your new major

4. Why would you <u>transfer</u> money?
   a. so it could be understood in many languages
   b. because it was changing
   c. to help the cashier make the correct change
   d. so you have enough money in your checking account to cover your expenses

5. Which of the following is an activity an <u>antisocial</u> person might like?
    a. going to a freshman orientation to meet new people
    b. attending a large Super Bowl party
    c. studying alone in the library
    d. studying with a large study group

6. Someone who is <u>antiestablishment</u> is <u>against</u> which of the following?
    a. the controlling group and the way things are currently organized
    b. change
    c. anything new that will change the way business is conducted
    d. fresh new ideas

7. When you use <u>antiseptic</u> hand wash, what do you hope to destroy?
    a. hamburger
    b. bad habits
    c. procrastination
    d. germs

8. An <u>antidote</u> for poor grades could be
    a. attending every class
    b. reviewing notes after every class
    c. studying ahead of time for exams
    d. all of the above

FILL IN THE BLANK   Select the BEST word for each sentence. Use each word only once.

transition	transmitted	antisocial	antiestablishment
transfer	transport	antiseptic	antidote

1. I had to go to the bank to _____ money from my savings account to my checking account.

2. Lisa knew that her mother sometimes felt _____ and argumentative, so she did not invite her to the open house at her new job.

3. Carol is a floor nurse in the local hospital. Every time she enters or leaves a patient's room she uses the _____ hand wash by the door to avoid spreading any germs.

4. Sue found that her younger child made an easy _____ from kindergarten to first grade.

5. Jeremy ran for election as the _____ candidate. He wanted to completely change the way the government was run.

6. The message was _____ to the space station by satellite.

7. The farmer needed a large truck to _____ the corn from his farm to the market.

8. After being bitten by a poisonous snake in the woods, Dale was rushed to the hospital in order to receive the _____.

CORRECT OR INCORRECT?   If the sentence is correct, write a "C" on the line provided. If not, write an "I" for incorrect, then REWRITE the sentence to make it correct. You can change any part of the sentence to make it correct.

1. I did not want to move from Ohio to Pennsylvania because I prefer a state of <u>transition</u>.

   _____

2. After Joe broke his hand, he had to get someone to <u>transmit</u> his lecture notes.

   _____

3. Joe was very <u>antisocial</u> and was invited to every party.

   _____

4. After she changed her major, Sally <u>transferred</u> to a new college.

   _____

5. In his government class Sam realized the professor held <u>antiestablishment</u> values because he was always praising the current administration and supported not changing any policies.

   _____

6. Sue is always worried about getting sick, so she has <u>antiseptic</u> hand gel in every room of her house and on her office desk.

   _____

7. Even though he knew it was illegal, Jerry tried to <u>transport</u> drugs across the state line.

   _____

8. Judy called the Poison Hotline to see whether the plant her dog ate was poisonous and whether there was an <u>antidote</u>.

   _____

SHORT ANSWER   Write your answers on a separate sheet of paper.

1. Describe a stage in your life when you had to make a difficult <u>transition</u>.
2. List two personality traits that would make you avoid an <u>antisocial</u> person.
3. Name two ways that we <u>transmit</u> information.
4. List two things that we <u>transfer</u>.
5. At your school, if you were the <u>antiestablishment</u> candidate for class president, what might your campaign platform be? Name three things.
6. Name three locations where you have seen a container or dispenser of <u>antiseptic</u> gel.
7. Name two ways you could <u>transport</u> textbooks.
8. What would be <u>antidotes</u> for the following situations?
   a. too many speeding tickets
   b. always being late for class and appointments
   c. getting lost around your town or campus
   d. no clean clothes to wear

Part B

WORDS TO LEARN—SEE AND SAY   Use the pronunciation guide on the first page of this book to help you SAY each word.

1. preface   prĕf′ĭs
2. preview   prē′vyōō′
3. prefix   prē′fĭks′
4. predict   prĭ-dĭkt′
5. precede   prĭ-sēd′
6. postpone   pōst-pōn′
7. postscript   pōst′skrĭpt′

STRUCTURAL ELEMENTS   Look at the structural elements of each word. Use these elements to unlock the word's meaning.

pre-   before
post-   after

 CONTEXT CLUES   Read the sentences. Use the words around the unfamiliar word to determine the word's meaning. Words in bold are the vocabulary words; words in italic are the context clues.

1. The **preface** to the Harry Potter book gives the reader an excellent idea of the author's purpose *before* he or she begins to read the book.

2. *Legally Blonde*, the movie, was just released this week; however, many privileged moviegoers were able to **preview** the movie weeks *before* the release.

3. By adding the **prefix** *auto-* to the base word *biography*, you change the meaning of the word to specifically mean "one's own life's story."

4. It is difficult to **predict** the *outcome* of Alfred Hitchcock's stories because he is an author who is an expert in keeping one in suspense.

5. A detailed account of who will be in the lineup, both on offense and the defense, will **precede** the game so the listeners *will know* who is playing *by the time the game begins*.

6. Dr. Miller **postponed** the *exam to next week* due to so many classes had been canceled because of the bad weather.

7. Jill added a **postscript** *at the end of the letter* to add something she had forgotten to write.

 DICTIONARY   Read the following definitions.

1. **preface**   prĕf′ĭs   noun

   Etymology: pre (before) fari (to speak)

   A preliminary statement or essay introducing a book that explains its scope, intention, or background and that is usually written by the author; words that come before the text's chapters

   After I read the **preface** *at the beginning of the book*, I understood the *author's purpose*.

   Something introductory

   An informal brunch served as a **preface** to the three-day conference.

   Synonyms: beginning, forward

   Antonym: appendix

   Vocabulary Tip: A *forward* is written by someone other than the author whereas a *preface* is generally written by the author or editor.

2. **preview**   prē′vyōō′   noun/verb

   Etymology: pre (before) view (see)

   (noun) An advance showing, as of a movie or exhibition

   Ms. Smith's third grade class attended the **preview** of the art exhibit *before it was opened* to the public.

   (verb) To view beforehand (as a textbook or other reading material)

   You should **preview** your textbook *to find the common elements in each chapter*.

   Synonyms: (verb) examine, show

3. **prefix**   prē′fĭks′   noun

   Etymology: pre (before) fix (fix)

   Something put or attached before something; an addition to

   By changing the **prefix** *at the beginning of a word* you can completely change the word's meaning.

   Synonyms: addition, affix

   Antonym: postscript

4. **predict**   prĭ-dĭkt′   verb

   Etymology: pre (before) dict (speak or say)

   To speak or tell in advance

   The weather forecasters were unable to **predict** with any accuracy the location of the hurricane *before it hit land.*

   Synonyms: forecast, anticipate

5. **precede**   prĭ-sēd′   verb

   Etymology: pre (before) cede (surrender)

   To come, exist, or occur before in time, in order or rank; to go in advance of

   It was necessary for the security personnel to **precede** the president into the conference room. They *entered first* to be sure it was safe for the president.

   Synonyms: antecede, predate, forerun

6. **postpone**   pōst-pōn′   verb

   Etymology: post (after) pon (put or place)

   To put off until another time

   The dance had to be **postponed** *for two weeks* due to the snowstorm that blanketed the city.

   Synonym: delay

   Antonyms: continue, persevere

7. **postscript**   pōst′skrĭpt′   noun

   Etymology: post (after) script (something written)

   Something written at the end of a book, letter, or essay that expresses a last thought

   After reading the **postscript** at *the end of the chapter*, the directions were much easier to follow.

   Synonyms: appendix, rider, footnote

Practice Exercises

MULTIPLE CHOICE

1. Which of the following have <u>previews</u>?
   a. movies
   b. restaurants
   c. late-model cars
   d. graduation ceremonies

2. Where would you find the <u>preface</u> in a book?
   a. at the beginning
   b. in the middle
   c. at the end
   d. on the Internet

3. Which of the following groups of words all have <u>prefixes</u>?
    a. critical, facial
    b. foot, hand, arm
    c. translate, reread
    d. past, prior, precede

4. When would you <u>predict</u> something?
    a. after the fact
    b. while it is happening
    c. before it happens
    d. none of the above

5. Which of the following would <u>not precede</u> earning a good grade on an exam?
    a. a high grade in the course
    b. monitoring your time while taking the exam
    c. reviewing your lecture notes several times a week
    d. making sure you did not skip any numbers on the answer sheet

6. Which of the following does <u>not</u> mean the same as <u>postpone</u>?
    a. hold off
    b. reschedule to a later date
    c. move forward
    d. delay

7. If you were writing a letter, where would a <u>postscript</u> be located?
    a. at the beginning
    b. in the middle
    c. at the end
    d. on the address label

FILL IN THE BLANK   Select the BEST word for each sentence. Use each word only once.

preface	previews	prefix	postponed
predict	preceded	postscript	

1. In the word *incorrect, in-* is a _____ added to the beginning of the word.

2. Because of the severe snowstorm, all of the schools were closed and the basketball game was _____.

3. I always read the _____ of my textbooks to find out the author's main focus for the book.

4. I like to get to the movies early so that I can see the _____ of coming attractions.

5. Janie was reading a letter her mother wrote to her father when he was in the military and was surprised to read a _____ at the end of the letter about her expected birth.

6. If I could _____ the future, I would know what jobs would be available when I graduate. That would help me pick my major.

7. The bridesmaids _____ the bride down the aisle.

CORRECT OR INCORRECT?   If the sentence is correct, write a "C" on the line provided. If not, write an "I" for incorrect, then REWRITE the sentence to make it correct. You can change any part of the sentence to make it correct.

1. The <u>preface</u> always comes at the end of the book.

_____

2. The <u>preview</u> at the end of the movie told the viewers what happened to the characters after the story ended.

_____

3. You can change the meaning of words by adding a <u>prefix</u> to the beginning.

_____

4. Jack and Jill were looking forward to their wedding day and were happy to <u>postpone</u> the ceremony.

_____

5. I like to visit with my old high school classmates and <u>predict</u> about our high school years.

_____

6. I didn't get much to eat because the people <u>preceding</u> me in the buffet line took all the food.

_____

7. Marie's job application cover letter started with a <u>postscript</u> about when she was available for an interview.

_____

SHORT ANSWER   Write your answers on a separate sheet of paper.

1. Why should you read the <u>preface</u> in your textbooks?
2. What do you look for when you <u>preview</u> a textbook chapter? List three things.
3. Look through this textbook and list three <u>prefixes</u> and their meanings.
4. Name three things you would like to <u>postpone</u>.
5. Besides a letter, what is something else that might have a <u>postscript</u>? Why?
6. What would you like to be able to <u>predict</u>? Explain your answer.
7. In the list A B C D E, what letter(s) <u>precede</u> *C?*

Power Words

1. **affiliation**   əfĭl′ē-ā′shən   noun

   Connections with other members of a group

   His **affiliation** with the club members gave him many good *business contacts.*

   Synonyms: coalition, conjunction

2. **excerpt**   ĕk′sûrpt′   noun

   A brief passage taken out of a larger text

   Because Sue only read an **excerpt** of the speech, she did *not understand the entire meaning.*

   Synonyms: passage, piece

3. **inference**   ĭn-fər-əns   noun

   A meaning that is not directly stated

   The **inference** that Sam took from the practical joke was that his friends did not like him, even though they *never directly said that.*

   Synonyms: implication, suggestion

Practice Exercises

1. Name three groups with which you have or would like to have an affiliation. Explain your connection to these groups.

2. What should you do if you copy an excerpt from a book into a paper for a class?

3. What inference would you make if someone winked at you from across the room?

Chapter Review

Matching

_____ 1. antisocial	a. helps prevent infection
_____ 2. transfer	b. to carry from one place to another
_____ 3. transmit	c. the introduction to a book
_____ 4. antidote	d. a word part that comes before a root word
_____ 5. transition	e. to put off until later
_____ 6. antiseptic	f. move from one form or style to another
_____ 7. transport	g. to come before something else
_____ 8. prefix	h. connection with members of a group
_____ 9. predict	i. to send from one person or place to another
_____10. postpone	j. a meaning not directly stated in the text
_____11. preface	k. stays away from the established social order
_____12. precede	l. to see or examine in advance
_____13. postscript	m. to say what will happen before the event
_____14. preview	n. to move from one location or job to another
_____15. affiliation	o. remedy for poison
_____16. excerpt	p. added to the end of a letter
_____17. inference	q. a brief passage from a larger text

Yes or No?

Read the sentence and answer the questions.

1. Sam read the preface when he was previewing his new history textbook.

   a. Did he examine the textbook before reading the assignment? _____

   b. Did he learn the author's purpose for writing the book? _____

2. Sue had predicted the previous five fires in her neighborhood.

   a. Did she know about the fires before they happened? _____

3. Joey was antisocial and avoided any affiliation with community groups.

   a. Did Joey like to socialize with people in the community? _____

   b. Was Joey a member of community groups in his neighborhood? _____

4. The paramedics gave Mary the antidote for the snake bite before transporting her to the hospital.

   a. Did the paramedics give Mary medicine? _____

   b. Did Mary drive herself to the hospital? _____

5. The <u>transfer</u> of money from Sally's saving account to her checking account was <u>preceded</u> by Mike's request to borrow money.

   a. Did Sally withdraw cash from her savings account? _____

   b. Did Mike ask for money after Sally transferred the funds? _____

6. Because Mike only read an <u>excerpt</u> from the <u>preface</u>, he made the wrong <u>inference</u> about the author's purpose.

   a. Did Mike read the entire preface? _____

   b. Did Mike try to reach a conclusion based on what he read? _____

Expanded Word Forms

transfer   transferred   transferal   affiliation   affiliated
predict   predicted   prediction

1. In order to _____ money from my savings to my checking account, I had to complete a _____ form. After the money was _____ I wrote checks to pay my bills.

2. I went to a fortune-teller at the circus to have my fortune told. Her _____ was crazy; she _____ that I would be a millionaire within two weeks. I don't really believe that anyone can _____ the future.

3. John's _____ with the professional baseball team was a dream come true. He had been _____ with other teams before, but not on the pro level.

Expand Your Learning

You learned in Chapter One that it is important to use a variety of strategies when learning and reviewing material. Do one or more of the following exercises to practice the words in this chapter.

Using your vision and color:

1. Write the words on note cards. Put the word on the front and the definition on the back. Use a different-color ink for the different categories of words according to the various word parts. To review the words, you should use three steps.
   a. Pronounce the word on the front.
   b. Try to remember the definition in your own words.
   c. Look at the back to check your answer.

   Separate the words into two piles, the ones you know and the ones you missed. Keep reviewing the ones you missed until you can recite them all correctly. You should repeat this several times during the week. Be sure to mix up the cards so you do not always do them in the same order.

2. Group the words according to their different word parts. Write each group in a different-color ink. Outline the shape of each word.

3. Draw simple stick figures to illustrate the meaning of each word.

4. Go back to the Fill in the Blank exercises and underline the context clues in each sentence that helped you identify the correct word.

5. Find other words that use the word parts in this chapter. Keep a list of words with each word part and add to it as you find more words throughout the semester.

Using your voice and hearing:

1. Make note cards as explained in the preceding exercise using vision. You do not need to use different-color inks unless you want to. When you go through the cards, say the words and the definitions out loud.

2. Go back to the Fill in the Blank exercises and read the sentences out loud. This would be a good way for you to check that you have used each word correctly.

Using large and small muscles (movement):

1. Fold a piece of paper in half lengthwise and label the columns A and B. Write the words in column A and the definitions in B. Fold back column A and recite the words from the definitions; then do the reverse. Review the words as you do some sort of physical activity such as walking or riding an exercise bike.

2. Put the words and definitions on note cards as explained in the preceding exercise using vision. You do not need to use different-color inks unless you want to. Carry these cards with you and review them throughout the day as you do your daily activities such as brushing your teeth, eating breakfast, etc.

Puzzle Fun

Word Scramble

Unscramble the vocabulary words. Write the definitions next to each word.

1. ainnstrtoi _____

2. dettnoia _____

3. aitstnrm _____

4. natpsiitce _____

5. ornspattr _____

6. htaitsbilsnmnetae _____

7. rsnaetfr _____

8. cioaalitns _____

9. ssoiptctpr _____

10. epstnoop _____

11. acfrepe _____

12. pxeifr _____

13. dtiprce _____

14. ierpewv _____

15. drpeeec _____

16. cterxep _____

17. eeennirfc _____

18. ftifnlaiiao _____

CHAPTER THREE
Using What You Know to Learn What You Don't Know

A word after a word after a word is power.

Margaret Atwood, Canadian Novelist (1939 –)

CHAPTER OBJECTIVE

Students will be able to identify and use words with the following common structural elements:

Prefixes: re-
Suffixes: -tion, -ion, -ic, -al

CHAPTER OUTLINE

 Memory Tip   Organize the Material to Be Learned

 Vocabulary Strategy   Word Structure

Part A
Words to Learn

react	reduce
relate	reinforce
revelation	retaliation
revolution	

Structural Elements

re-	-tion, -ion

Part B
Words to Learn

critical	thematic
logical	facial
aerobic	exotic
residential	

Structural Elements

-ic	-al

Power Words

appropriate	pessimist
organic	optimist

Memory Tip   Organize the Material to Be Learned

The second step in learning is to organize the information in some logical format. In this book the words are organized according to structural elements. The seven to nine words you are learning in each section are organized around two or three structural elements.

This carries over into your other studies and courses. Before reading a textbook chapter, preview it to see how the author has organized the material. In your other courses, look at the syllabus to see how the professor has organized the course. When attending a lecture, look for the professor's organization.

Whatever it is that you are learning, it will be easier and more meaningful if you understand the organization or organize the material yourself.

 Vocabulary Strategy   Word Structure

Many words have structural elements that will help you to unlock the meaning. There are three structural elements:

- prefix (added at the beginning of the word)
- suffix (added at the end of the word)
- root (base)

Most often prefixes have specific meanings. For example, the word *script* means "a text or something written," and by adding the prefix *post-* to the word it becomes *postscript,* "something that is written at the end."

A suffix can change a word from an adjective to a noun or from an adjective to an adverb. Here are some examples of words that are altered by adding a suffix:

- comic (noun)   comic**al** (adjective)   comic**ally** (adverb)
- react (verb)   reac**tion** (noun)
- reinforce (verb)   reinforce**ment** (noun)

A root is also called a *base,* the part of the word that we start with before adding a prefix or suffix. In the preceding example, *comic, react,* and *reinforce* are the root or base words.

Part A

   WORDS TO LEARN—SEE AND SAY   Use the pronunciation guide on the first page of this book to help you SAY each word.

1. react   rē-ăkt′
2. reduce   rĭ-dōōs′
3. relate   rĭ-lāt′
4. reinforce   rē′in-fôrs′
5. revelation   rĕv′ə-lā′shən
6. revolution   rĕv′ə-lōō′shən
7. retaliation   ri-′ta-lē-′āt- shən

   STRUCTURAL ELEMENTS   Look at the structural elements of each word. Use these elements to unlock the word's meaning.

re- (prefix)   back, again

-tion, -ion (suffixes)   act, state, or condition of

   CONTEXT CLUES   Read the sentences. Use the words around the unfamiliar word to determine the word's meaning. Words in bold are the vocabulary words; words in italic are the context clues.

1. Every time I asked A.J. a question, he would **react** *by getting angry.*

2. The main reason for the plan is to **reduce** the amount of money that is being spent each month *to a lower, more reasonable figure.*

3. Although the movie and the book seem **related** because they *share the same* title, the story is quite different.

4. To build a positive attitude in children, it is necessary to **reinforce** that attitude *with praise every time a child responds appropriately.*

5. It was a **revelation,** an *unveiling* of sorts, that the mother saw when her son returned from his freshman year in college. She found him to be a mature young man instead of a flighty, immature boy.

6. In math class we had to figure out how many **revolutions** a tire made in one minute. The teacher told us how long it took for the tire to complete one *cycle.*

7. The *ruler in power was overthrown* by the antiestablishment party during the **revolution.**

8. John **retaliated** by sulking in his room and not eating dinner as a way of *getting back at* his parents for grounding him for one week.

 DICTIONARY   Read the following definitions.

1. **react**   rē-ăkt′   verb

   Etymology: re (back, again) act

   To act in response to, or under the influence of, a stimulus or prompt

   Mia **reacted** *strongly to* the sarcastic tone of the memorandum.

   Synonyms: reply, answer

2. **reduce**   rĭ-dōōs′   verb

   Etymology: re (back, again) duc (to lead)

   To bring down, as in extent, amount, or degree; diminish

   Deandra was *very upset* and **reduced** *to tears* when she got the news of the accident.

   Synonyms: abridge, curtail

   Antonyms: expand, extend

3. **relate**   rĭ-lāt′   verb

   Etymology: re (back, again) ate (to make or cause to be)

   To narrate or tell; to establish or demonstrate a connection between

   Lisa said that she was not able to **relate** to her college classmates *because she had been out of school for fifteen years and was much older.*

   Synonyms: depict, describe

4. **reinforce**   rē′ĭn-fôrs′   verb

   Etymology: re (back, again) inforce (variation on the word *enforce*)

   To give more force or effectiveness to; strengthen

   The news of the plant relocation **reinforced** *and strengthened* her hopes of getting a promotion.

   Synonyms: augment, emphasize

   Antonym: decrease

5. **revelation**   rĕv′ ə-lā′shən   noun

   Etymology: re (back, again) vel (veil) tion (act, state, or condition of)

   A pleasant surprise; a disclosure

When the story was *reported on the evening news,* the **revelation** of the popular mayor's decision to run for president was a *surprise* to everyone in the city.

Synonyms: discovery, epiphany

Antonym: secret

Vocabulary Tip: A revelation is generally a pleasant happening.

6.   **revolution**   rĕv′ə-lōō′shən   noun

Etymology: re (back) vol (turn) tion (act, state, or condition of)

Turning or rotational motion about an axis

The **revolution**, *or rotation,* of the earth takes one year to complete.

The overthrow of one's government and its replacement with another

During the **revolution** the *old government was overthrown* and a new leader put in place.

Synonyms: rotation, rebellion

7.   **retaliation**   ri-′ta-lē-′āt- shən   noun

Etymology: re (back) talio (such like)

To deliberately hurt or do something harmful to someone because that person has done something harmful to you first

He felt that seeking **retaliation** *for the evil act* was beneath him and opted to forgive instead.

Synonyms: revenge, payback

Practice Exercises

MULTIPLE CHOICE

1. In which situation might someone <u>react</u> by crying?
    a. earning an "A" on an exam
    b. watching a sad movie
    c. walking the dog
    d. sweeping the rug

2. Why would you <u>reduce</u> your driving speed?
    a. to pass a slow moving car
    b. to get home faster
    c. because you are in a construction zone
    d. because you want to test your new car

3. Which of the following are <u>related</u>?
    a. bagels, buns, and bread
    b. horses and tennis rackets
    c. paper, rocks, and tennis balls
    d. cars, textbooks, and paperclips

4. Which of the following could you use to <u>reinforce</u> a button on your shirt?
    a. scissors
    b. a nail file
    c. needle and thread
    d. Scotch tape and masking tape

5. A word or phrase that means the same as <u>revelation</u> is
   a. a secret
   b. something that is concealed
   c. an unveiling
   d. a person of distinction

6. Which of the following means the same as <u>revolution</u>?
   a. overthrow
   b. rotation
   c. cycle
   d. all of the above
   e. none of the above

7. Which of the following would someone say if he or she wanted <u>retaliation</u>?
   a. "Could you do me a favor?"
   b. "Let me help you with that."
   c. "You dropped your wallet."
   d. "I'll get you for that."

FILL IN THE BLANK   Select the BEST word for each sentence. Use each word only once.

react	reduce	relate	reinforced
revelation	revolutions	retaliation	

1. The young mother _____ her command to set the table by handing the child the placemats and napkins.

2. The history professor wanted his students to _____ the information in the movie to the information from his class lecture.

3. The college put timers on the showers that made them shut off after ten minutes in order to _____ the amount of water used and lower the water bill.

4. At the science day at the amusement park the physics class had to measure the number of _____ each bench made during a typical ride on the Ferris wheel.

5. How do you _____ when you see a big dog? I walk in the opposite direction because I do not like dogs.

6. It was a complete _____ to Joe when he realized that he was expected to study on his own outside of class.

7. After the high school's football championship, the losing team painted the statue of the winning team's mascot in _____.

CORRECT OR INCORRECT?   If the sentence is correct, write a "C" on the line provided. If not, write an "I" for incorrect, then REWRITE the sentence to make it correct. You can change any part of the sentence to make it correct.

1. I <u>reduced</u> the number of calories in my diet by eating more junk food.

   _____

2. Sue knew so little about cars that it was a <u>revelation</u> to her that she needed to change the oil.

   _____

3. The policeman <u>reinforced</u> the seriousness of the offense when he did not give the driver a ticket for running the red light.

   _____

4. Sue <u>reacted</u> with a sigh of relief when she opened her SAT test results.

_____

5. Brenda can <u>relate</u> her high grades to her improved study habits.

_____

6. In <u>retaliation</u> for Jenna gossiping about her, Sue sent Jenna flowers.

_____

7. The antiestablishment party planned a complete <u>revolution</u> of the party in power.

_____

SHORT ANSWER   Write your answers on a separate sheet of paper.

1. Describe your <u>reaction</u> to a horror movie.
2. How could you <u>reduce</u> the number of parking tickets you receive?
3. Describe two ways a professor might <u>reinforce</u> the information that will be on the exam.
4. Name three different ways you can be <u>related</u> to someone.
5. What is one <u>revelation</u> you have had about yourself since taking this or another course?
6. Name three things that have <u>revolutions</u> you can measure. Examples would be the tires on a car or the latest government overthrow around the world.
7. <u>Retaliation</u> has a negative mearning. What are three positive reactions you could have when someone does or says something negatiave to you?

Part B

 WORDS TO LEARN—SEE AND SAY   Use the pronunciation guide on the first page of this book to help you SAY each word.

1.	critical	krĭt′ĭ-kəl
2.	thematic	thĭ-măt′ĭk
3.	logical	lŏj′ĭ-kəl
4.	facial	fā′shəl
5.	aerobic	â-rō′bĭk
6.	exotic	ĭg-zŏt′ĭk
7.	residential	rĕz′ĭ-dĕn′shəl

 STRUCTURAL ELEMENTS   Look at the structural elements of each word. Use these elements to unlock the word's meaning.

-ic   relates to, pertains to

-al   relates to, pertains to

CONTEXT CLUES   Read the sentences. Use the words around the unfamiliar word to determine the word's meaning. Words in bold are the vocabulary words; words in italic are the context clues.

1. It would be a **critical** error to drink and drive; the _consequences can be life changing._

2. After years of writing novels, the author is known as a spiritual writer because the **thematic** approach that he takes _in all of his books_ deals with the spiritual renewal of life.

3. With dark clouds and mild winds, rain was the **logical** *expectation,* given the time of year.

4. Although Alyssa said that she enjoyed the concert, *her* **facial** *expression* indicated just the opposite.

5. Most doctors recommend an exercise program that incorporates a good diet, plenty of rest, and at least three days of **aerobic** exercise per week to improve the *oxygen flow* in the blood.

6. A flamingo is an **exotic** bird that is *not found in any place* in the United States except zoos or aviaries.

7. **Residential** codes are established to protect the *homeowner* when *building a new house.* These codes are in place to ensure safety.

 DICTIONARY   Read the following definitions.

1. **critical**   krĭt′ĭ-kəl   adjective

   Etymology: critic (crucial) al (relates to or pertains to)

   Inclined to judge severely and find fault

   Jesse's **critical** *evaluation* of the employee *resulted in the employee's dismissal.*

   Characterized by careful, exact evaluation and judgment

   It is important to learn to be a **critical** reader and thinker in college and to be able to carefully *understand and evaluate* what you are learning.

   Indispensable; essential

   The **critical** point *that determined the outcome* of the case was when the weapon was found.

   Synonyms: derogatory, demeaning, careful, essential

   Antonyms: complimentary, laudable

2. **thematic**   thĭ-măt′ĭk   adjective

   Etymology: theme (root) ic (relates to or pertains to)

   Relating to a theme or topic

   The designer created a **topical** atmosphere by adding tropical plants and animal print fabric, so that the guests *felt as though they were in a jungle setting.*

   Synonym: subject

3. **logical**   lŏj′ĭ-kəl   adjective

   Etymology: logic (root) al (relates to or pertains to)

   Reasonable, or capable of reasoning in a clear and consistent manner

   There was a *good reason* that it was **logical** to expect that Bill would get a speeding ticket. He always drove over the speed limit.

   Synonyms: coherent, congruent

   Antonyms: incoherent, unlikely

4. **facial**   fā′shəl   adjective/noun

   Etymology: face (root) al (relates to or pertains to)

   (adjective) Of or concerning the face

   Her **facial** *expression* clearly showed her surprise.

   (noun) A treatment for the face, usually consisting of a massage and the application of cosmetic creams

   After being given a cucumber **facial,** the young girl experienced an allergic reaction and broke out in hives all over *her face.*

5. **aerobic** â-rō′bĭk adjective

   Etymology: aero (oxygen) ic (relates to or pertains to)

   Involving or improving oxygen consumption by the body

   The doctor told Alyssa to start doing some **aerobic** exercise in order to *increase her heart rate and strengthen her lungs and heart.*

   Antonym: anaerobic

   Vocabulary Tip: Most of the time this word is connected to exercise that increases the rate at which your body uses oxygen.

6. **exotic** ĭg-zŏt′ĭk adjective

   Etymology: ex (out, outside) ic (relates to or pertains to)

   From another part of the world; foreign; intriguingly unusual or different

   The **exotic** dancers from Pakistan performed at the *International Dance Festival.*

   Synonym: extraordinary

   Antonyms: normal, ordinary, familiar

   Vocabulary Tip: Anything strange, unusual, or unknown can be considered exotic. The word generally has a positive connotation such as in "an exotic, or tropical, vacation."

7. **residential** rĕz′ĭ-dĕn′shəl adjective

   Etymology: resid (resident, house) al (relates to or pertains to)

   Relating to having a home

   University State is a **residential** college; *housing is provided for students* if they request it.

Practice Exercises

MULTIPLE CHOICE

1. A <u>critical</u> reader would
   a. skim the material for the basic facts
   b. evaluate the author's information
   c. look for the bold print words
   d. just do the questions at the end of the chapter

2. If a teacher is developing a <u>thematic</u> unit, he or she might include
   a. several types of information on the same topic
   b. material on a wide variety of subjects
   c. one large reading assignment
   d. only one book on the subject

3. If you are a <u>logical</u> thinker, you
   a. let your mind wander all over the place
   b. do things in any order that you wish
   c. do not plan ahead
   d. think in an orderly manner

4. If you get a <u>facial</u>, you
    a. go to a garage and have your oil changed
    b. go to the movies to see *Face Off*
    c. go to a salon and have your skin cleansed and moisturized
    d. go to the local park and have a face-off between two teams

5. Which of the following is <u>aerobic</u> exercise?
    a. lifting weights
    b. watching a movie on TV
    c. shopping
    d. jogging

6. An animal would be considered <u>exotic</u> if
    a. it was commonly found in your local area
    b. it was unusual
    c. it had a funny name that is hard to pronounce
    d. it was attractive

7. What would you find in a <u>residential</u> area?
    a. stores and bus stops
    b. businesses and parking lots
    c. tourist sites and tour buses
    d. houses and children

FILL IN THE BLANK   Select the BEST word for each sentence. Use each word only once.

critical	thematic	logical	facial
aerobic	exotic	residential	

1. The amusement park was _____ because all the rides and games related to comic book characters.

2. The pleasant way she smiled added to her pleasing _____ expression.

3. I am a very _____ person, so when I have a job to do I usually plan it out step by step.

4. The _____ mother did not like anything her children did.

5. _____ exercise is important to keep your heart healthy.

6. I live in a(n) _____ area, so there are always neighbors nearby when I need to borrow something.

7. The pet store specialized in _____ animals that could not naturally be found in the surrounding areas.

CORRECT OR INCORRECT?   If the sentence is correct, write a "C" on the line provided. If not, write an "I" for incorrect, then REWRITE the sentence to make it correct. You can change any part of the sentence to make it correct.

1. The teacher was very <u>critical</u> of her students and praised everything that they did in class.

_____

2. I like to work in <u>thematic</u> units, so everything we read can be related to the other material.

_____

3. If you are a very <u>logical</u> and orderly person, you usually do not follow directions or do things in the most obvious order.

_____

4. Sue was very upset about her <u>facial</u> scar that was the result of her broken arm.

_____

5. I go to the gym several days a week to do some <u>aerobic</u> exercise, like jogging on the treadmill.

_____

6. Earthworms are wild and <u>exotic</u> creatures.

_____

7. The <u>residential</u> area in downtown Chicago has streets lined with shops and restaurants, but no one really lives there.

_____

SHORT ANSWER   Write your answers on a separate sheet of paper.

1. What does it mean to be a <u>critical</u> reader?

2. What might be included in a <u>thematic</u> study of your state?

3. How would you determine if an answer to a mathematical problem were <u>logical</u>?

4. If you are studying someone's <u>facial</u> expression, what are you looking for?

5. Name three types of <u>aerobic</u> exercise. Why is aerobic exercise good for your health?

6. Name three <u>exotic</u> animals. Why would they be considered exotic?

7. Think of an ideal <u>residential</u> area. What three characteristics or services are included?

Power Words

1. **appropriate**   ə-prō′prē-ĭt   adjective

   Suitable for a particular person, condition, occasion, or place; fitting

   What is the **appropriate** dress to wear for the formal dance? *I don't want to be dressed differently than the other guests.*

   appropriate   ə-prō′prē-āt′   verb

   To set apart for a specific use; to take possession of or make use of exclusively for oneself, often without permission

   Lee **appropriated** my unread newspaper *and never returned it.*

   Synonyms: (adj) suitable, fitting; (verb) allot, assign, budget

2. **organic**   ôr-găn′ĭk   adjective

   Relating to or derived from living organisms; relating to or affecting a bodily organ

   Tom preferred **organic** vegetables because he *did not want to eat the chemicals sprayed on food to kill pests.*

   Synonyms: essential, elemental, basic

   Antonyms: man-made, unnatural

3. **optimist**   ŏp′tə-mĭst   noun

    One who usually expects a favorable outcome

    Darlene was always an **optimist**; she could *always see the bright side* of any situation.

    Synonym: enthusiast

4. **pessimist**   pĕs′a-mĭst   noun

    One who usually expects an unfavorable outcome

    Saul was a **pessimist** when discussing his performance on the exam; he *expected to fail*.

    Synonym: doomsayer

    Vocabulary Tip: Winston Churchill once said, "A pessimist sees the difficulty in every opportunity; the optimist see the opportunity in every difficulty."

Practice Exercises

1. Write three words to describe an optimist and three to describe a pessimist.

2. Use the word organic in a sentence.

3. What would be the appropriate dress for these occasions?
    a. the beach
    b. a funeral
    c. a wedding

Chapter Review

Yes or No?

Read the sentence and answer the questions.

1. Sam reacted to his large debt by reducing the amount of money he spent on entertainment.

    a. Did Sam ignore the large amount of money he owed people? _____

    b. Did Sam begin to spend less money? _____

2. Jim was an optimist and was surprised when Carol retaliated after he broke up with her.

    a. Did Jim think the worst would happen? _____

    b. Did Carol react to the breakup in a positive way? _____

3. Joe was pessimistic about the results of his aerobic exercise program to reduce his weight.

    a. Did Joe feel positive about his exercise program? _____

    b. Was Joe lifting weights to build muscle? _____

    c. Did Joe want to lose weight? _____

4. The professor had a logical plan for the class and presented all the material in thematic units.

    a. Was the professor's plan well thought out? _____

    b. Were the units organized around one controlling idea? _____

5. The exotic monkey had very unusual facial features.

    a. Was the monkey commonly found in the area? _____

    b. Were the monkey's hands and feet different? _____

6. The <u>appropriate</u> speed when driving through a <u>residential</u> area is usually 25 mph.

   a. Is 25 mph the correct speed to drive? _____

   b. Would you be driving by factories? _____

Related Forms

Add the suffix *-tion* or *-ion* to the following words to change their meaning. Write sentences using the new forms of the words. You can check you answers with a classmate or dictionary.

1. react

2. reduce

3. relate

Expanded Word Forms

reaction	reacts	react	reduced	reduction
reinforce	reinforced	reinforcements		

1. Everyone _____ differently when a cute dog jumps up on him or her. Some people's _____ is to pet the dog, but others _____ by pushing the dog away.

2. Do you think the price of gas will ever be _____? A _____ of ten cents per gallon would really help out my budget.

3. General Smith hoped to _____ the strength of his troops and win the battle. The _____ arrived just as his soldiers were thinking about surrendering. The _____ troops were finally able to overcome the enemy.

Expand Your Learning

You learned in Chapter One that it is important to use a variety of strategies when learning and reviewing material. Do one or more of the following exercises to practice the words in this chapter.

Using your vision and color:

1. Write the words on note cards. Put the word on the front and the definition on the back. Use a different-color ink for the different categories of words according to the various word parts. To review the words, you should use three steps.
   a. Pronounce the word on the front.
   b. Try to remember the definition in your own words.
   c. Look at the back to check your answer.

   Separate the words into two piles, the ones you know and the ones you missed. Keep reviewing the ones you missed until you can recite them all correctly. You should repeat this several times during the week. Be sure to mix up the cards so you do not always do them in the same order.

2. Group the words according to their different word parts. Write each group in a different-color ink. Outline the shape of each word.

3. Draw simple stick figures to illustrate the meaning of each word.

4. Go back to the Fill in the Blank exercises and underline the context clues in each sentence that helped you identify the correct word.

5. Find other words that use the word parts in this chapter. Keep a list of words with each word part and add to it as you find more words throughout the semester.

Using your voice and hearing:

1. Make note cards as explained in the preceding exercise using vision. You do not need to use different-color inks unless you want to. When you go through the cards, say the words and the definitions out loud.

2. Go back to the Fill in the Blank exercises and read the sentences out loud. This would be a good way for you to check that you have used each word correctly.

Using large and small muscles:

1. Fold a piece of paper in half lengthwise and label the columns A and B. Write the words in column A and the definitions in B. Fold back column A and recite the words from the definitions; then do the reverse. Review the words as you do some sort of physical activity such as walking or riding an exercise bike.

2. Put the words and definitions on note cards as explained in the preceding exercise using vision. You do not need to use different-colors inks unless you want to. Carry these cards with you and review them throughout the day as you do your daily activities such as brushing your teeth, eating breakfast, etc.

Puzzle Fun

Across
3. relating to the face
8. from another part of the world; foreign
10. relating to a given topic
11. relating to or derived from living organisms
12. involving oxygen consumption by the body
14. to act in response to
15. relating to the home
16. something that is made known

Down
1. one who expects a favorable outcome
2. inclined to judge severely and find fault
4. suitable
5. to bring down or diminish
6. acting in a clear and consistent manner
7. establish a connection between
9. one who expects a negative outcome
13. strengthen

CHAPTER FOUR

Working with Context Clues

Learning is a treasure that accompanies its owners everywhere.

Chinese proverb

CHAPTER OBJECTIVE

Students will be able to identify and use words with the following common structural elements:

Root: graph

Prefixes: im-, in-, il-, ir-, de-

CHAPTER OUTLINE

 Memory Tip   Test/Retest

 Vocabulary Strategy   Context Clues Part I

Part A
Words to Learn

irregular	illegal
irrelevant	illogical
improper	inconsistent
immoral	infuriate

Structural Elements

im-, in-, il-, ir-

Part B
Words to Learn

decline	telegraph
detract	graphology
deplete	graphic
deactivate	

Structural Elements

de-   graph

Power Words

surpass	poise
inhale	

Memory Tip   Test/Retest

Learning requires more than just repetition. You have to test your memory—practice restating the information purely from memory, without looking at the material. One way to do this with your vocabulary words is to put them on study cards—the word on the front and the definition on the back. Then do this:

- Look at the word

- Think about the definition

- Check yourself

- Set the ones aside that you do not know and then keep going over them until you get them correct

Of course you can also do the reverse: look at the definition and remember the word.

The possibilities for using this learning strategy in your other classes are endless. In addition to study cards, you can review your notes, cover them up and restate the information, and then check yourself. Do the same with your textbooks; read a section, close your book and restate what you read, then check yourself. You can make practice tests, set them aside, and take them in a few days. What else can you think of?

 ## *Vocabulary Strategy*   Context Clues Part I

Comprehension is dependent on understanding the words the author uses; therefore, it is helpful to use the author's words to help you understand. The words around the unfamiliar one are often context clues that can help you comprehend the unknown word. In this book, after the pronunciation and structural elements, the words are presented in sentences using clear context cues to help you define the word on your own as you would when you are reading.

Common context clues that authors use when writing college textbooks are:

- definition

- restatement or synonyms

- examples

- contrast/antonyms

- cause and effect

In this chapter you will review the first three from the preceding list.

When using the context clue of *definition* the writer will put the definition directly in the sentence. The writer will signal the definition by using words such as:

- any form of the verb *to be* (*is, am, are,* etc.)

- *that is*

- *to be called*

- *refers to*

- *means*

- punctuation marks such as commas, dashes, etc.

Context clues of *restatement* simply illustrate the unfamiliar word by also using a synonym.

When using the context clue of restatement you will see signal words such as:

- *that is*

- *or*

- *in other words*

The third type of context clues is *example* where by the author adds an example of the word in the sentence. Words that signal examples may be:

- *as*

- *including*

- *such as*

- *for instance*
- *for example*
- *especially*
- punctuation marks such as colons and parentheses

As you are reading the Context Clues sections in this chapter, pay attention to how the writer draws your attention to the new word.

Part A

 WORDS TO LEARN—SEE AND SAY   Use the pronunciation guide on the first page of this book to help you SAY each word.

1. irregular   ĭ-rĕg′yə-lər
2. irrelevant   ĭ-rĕl′ə-vənt
3. immoral   ĭ-môr′əl
4. improper   ĭm-prŏp′ər
5. illegal   ĭ-lē′gəl
6. illogical   ĭ-lŏj′ĭ-kəl
7. inconsistent   n′kən-sĭs′tənt
8. infuriate   ĭn-fyŏŏr′ē-āt′

 STRUCTURAL ELEMENTS   Look at the structural elements of each word. Use these elements to unlock the word's meaning.

im-, in-, il-, ir-   not

CONTEXT CLUES   Read the sentences. Use the words around the unfamiliar word to determine the word's meaning. Words in bold are the vocabulary words; words in italic are context clues.

1. The **irregular** road surface *jolted the car with every bump of the crumbled pavement.*
2. Joe's comment was **irrelevant** to the discussion and *did not add anything to the information* needed.
3. *Stealing* from your company or from your friends is an **immoral** act that could be punished by arrest and conviction for theft.
4. Many businesses consider it **improper,** *not acceptable,* to wear shorts and sandals to work.
5. It is both *immoral* and **illegal** to *steal* money from your place of employment.
6. It is **illogical** *to think you can never study and still earn an A* on an exam.
7. His *mean* comment was **inconsistent** with Sam's *kind nature.* He always said kind things to others.
8. Finding litter in her yard **infuriated** Sally. It always made her *very angry* every time she had to pick up what people threw from their cars.

 DICTIONARY   Read the following definitions.

1. **irregular**   ĭ-rĕg′yə-lər   adjective

   Etymology: ir (not) regular

   Not straight, uniform, or symmetrical

Valerie's haircut was **irregular** because *the left side was longer than the right side.*

Synonym: inconsistent

Antonyms: regular, consistent

2. **irrelevant** ǐ-rĕl'ə-vənt   adjective

Etymology: ir (not) relevant (related to)

Unrelated to the matter being considered

The **irrelevant** information that was in the article *confused the main point* the reporter was trying to get his readers to understand.

Synonyms: immaterial, unrelated

Antonym: necessary

3. **immoral** ǐ-môr'əl   adjective

Etymology: im (not) mor (behavior) al (relates to or pertains to)

Violating the behavior of something that is right or wrong

Many people argue that abortion is **immoral** and definitely a *terribly wrong* action.

Synonym: unscrupulous

Antonyms: good, moral

Vocabulary Tip: Something or someone who is **immoral** knows the difference between right and wrong, which is different from something or someone who is *amoral. Amoral* describes something that has no morals and doesn't know what right or wrong means.

4. **improper** ǐm-prŏp'ər   adjective

Etymology: im (not) proper

Not suitable or right according to accepted standards of social or professional behavior

Wearing blue jeans to a formal wedding would be considered grossly **improper** attire.

Synonym: inappropriate

Antonyms: fitting, proper

5. **illegal** ǐ-lē'gəl   adjective

Etymology: il (not) leg (law) al (relates to or pertains to)

Prohibited by law

It is **illegal** to *take guns and knives on an airplane.*

Synonym: outlawed

Antonym: lawful

6. **illogical** ǐ-lŏj'ǐ-kəl   adjective

Etymology: il (not) logic; al (relates to or pertains to)

Contradicting the laws of logic or reasoning; not based on clear facts or principles

Most people would consider it **illogical** to try to argue their own case in a court of law because you need to *understand the principles* of law and the order of the courtroom as well.

Synonym: incoherent

Antonyms: coherent; understandable

7. **inconsistent**   n′kən-sĭs′tənt   adjective

Etymology: in (not) consistent

Not uniform or the same throughout

When one psychologist does an experiment and gets one result and another psychologist does the same experiment and gets *different results,* the results are said to be **inconsistent**.

Synonyms: irregular, changeable; contrary

Antonyms: consistent; unchanging

8. **infuriate**   ĭn-fyŏŏr′ē-āt′   verb

Etymology: often the **prefix** *in-* is negative and means "not" (e.g., invalid = not valid). However, there are also instances like here, where *in-* is actually part of the original root word and denotes a stronger meaning

To make furious or enraged

Ringing cell phones during class **infuriates** Dr. Miller, so the students turn their phones off so they do not make her *angry.*

Synonyms: to anger; to aggravate

Antonym: to please

Practice Exercises

MULTIPLE CHOICE

1. Which of the following is an <u>irregular</u> pattern?
   a. 1, 2, 1, 2, 1, 2
   b. 1, 2, 3, 4, 5, 6, 7
   c. 4, 6, 8, 10, 12, 14
   d. 3, 8, 5, 1, 7, 2

2. If you make an <u>irrelevant</u> comment it is
   a. not about the topic of conversation
   b. right on target
   c. an important addition to the information discusssed
   d. reinforcing what someone just said

3. Which of the following means the opposite of <u>improper</u>?
   a. rude
   b. impolite
   c. suitable
   d. inappropriate

4. Which of the following describes someone who is <u>immoral</u>?
   a. commits crimes against society
   b. helps elderly people across the street
   c. shovels his or her neighbors' driveways
   d. shakes hands when he or she first meets someone

5. Which of the following means the same as <u>illegal</u>?
   a. unlawful
   b. retaliation
   c. revolution
   d. illogical

6. Which of the following could be <u>illogical</u>?
   a. your explanation about why you were driving above the speed limit
   b. your career goal
   c. your answer to an essay question
   d. all of the above

7. An <u>inconsistent</u> response or reaction would mean that
   a. everything proceeds as planned
   b. you do not know what to expect
   c. the response is illegal
   d. the same thing will happen as the last time

8. Which of the following is the opposite of <u>infuriate</u>?
   a. to make calm
   b. to enrage
   c. to inspire
   d. to help understand

FILL IN THE BLANK   Select the BEST word for each sentence. Use each word only once.

irregular	irrelevant	immoral	improper
illegal	illogical	inconsistent	infuriated

NOTE: Two of the words can be used in either of two sentences.

1. The fact that Miles did not want to go to bed was _____ in his mother's opinion. It was his bedtime and she was making the decision.

2. My dog's behavior is very _____. I can never predict how he will act.

3. The man was so _____ by his neighbor's dog's constant barking that he called the police.

4. It was _____ for Sammy to buy a little convertible sports car when she lived in an area where there was always a lot of snow.

5. Jamie was very _____ about his bedtime. Sometimes he went to bed at 9:00 PM and sometimes at 1:00 or 2:00 AM.

6. Talking when others are talking and talking with your mouth full are examples of _____ behavior.

7. Sam was arrested because of his _____ activities.

8. Even though he did not break the law, Mark's _____ behavior caused him to lose many friends as well as his job.

CORRECT OR INCORRECT?   If the sentence is correct, write a "C" on the line provided. If not, write an "I" for incorrect, then REWRITE the sentence to make it correct. You can change any part of the sentence to make it correct.

1. Mark is being treated for an <u>irregular</u> heartbeat. His doctors are trying to get it back to its normal rhythm.

   _____

2. Jim's comment was <u>irrelevant</u> to the discussion and did not add any new information.

   _____

3. Jenny wanted to always act in an <u>improper</u> way, so she was polite to everyone she met.

_____

4. Jane was recognized for her <u>immoral</u> behavior and named "Volunteer of the Year."

_____

5. Driving over the speed limit is considered <u>illegal</u> and will result in a fine and ticket if caught.

_____

6. Joyce was very clear and orderly in her thinking; therefore, her explanation was <u>illogical</u>.

_____

7. The student teacher's classroom management techniques were <u>inconsistent</u> with the supervising teacher's, so the students were confused and did not know what to expect.

_____

8. I have a very mild-mannered, laid-back personality, so there are many things that <u>infuriate</u> me.

_____

SHORT ANSWER   Write your answers on a separate sheet of paper.

1. List three things that you regularly do. How could you do them <u>irregularly</u>? One example is the way you get to class—your regular route and an irregular route.

2. Think about how you spend your time during a normal week. What activities are <u>irrelevant</u> to your academic success and daily basic needs? What activities are relevant to the same?

3. Name two behaviors in the classroom that are <u>improper</u> and two that are proper.

4. Name three <u>immoral</u> acts.

5. How are the meanings of the words <u>illegal</u> and <u>immoral</u> similar? Are they different in any way?

6. Name two decisions that are <u>illogical</u>, but not <u>illegal</u>.

7. How would a two-year-old's behavior be <u>inconsistent</u> with what his mother would want? Name two ways.

8. Name two things that <u>infuriate</u> you.

Part B

WORDS TO LEARN—SEE AND SAY   Use the pronunciation guide on the first page of this book to help you SAY each word.

1. decline   dĭ-klīn'

2. deplete   dĭ-plēt'

3. detract   dĭ-trăkt'

4. deactivate   dē-ăk'tə-vāt'

5. telegraph   tĕl'ĭ-grăf'

6. graphology   gră-fŏl'ə-jē

7. graphic   grăf'ĭk

STRUCTURAL ELEMENTS   Look at the structural elements of each word. Use these elements to unlock the word's meaning.

de-   down or away; apart

graph   something written

 CONTEXT CLUES   Read the sentences. Use the words around the unfamiliar word to determine the word's meaning. Words in bold are the vocabulary words; words in italic are the context clues.

1. I regretfully **decline**; I *will not accept* the offer to sit on the board of directors.

2. After one semester in college, Emily **depleted** her college account. She had to resort to taking out *school loans and relying on school grants.*

3. The loud music only **detracted**—*took away from*—the seriousness of the speaker's message.

4. Sue **deactivated** the television remote when she *turned off* the electrical power in the house.

5. Long before the telephone was invented, messages were sent by **telegraph** *over electrical lines in the form of coded signals.*

6. Dr. Jones became famous for his skills in **graphology** when he was able to *identify two serial killers through their handwriting.*

7. The **graphic** novel contained *pictures* as well as *words* to *help the reader visualize the details* of the story.

 DICTIONARY   Read the following definitions.

1. **decline**   dǐ-klīn′   verb/noun

   Etymology: de (down, apart, away, off) cline (to bend)

   (verb) To express polite refusal

   I regretfully **decline** the nomination due to previous commitments. I *cannot take on the job* at this time.

   (noun) A downward movement

   The **decline** in the job market forced many young people to move out of the state because they *could not find jobs.*

   Synonyms: (verb) abstain; (noun) downturn

   Antonyms: (verb) accept; (noun) improvement

2. **deplete**   dǐ-plēt′   verb

   Etymology: de (down, apart, away, off) plere (to fill)

   To decrease the fullness of; use up

   Since the campers' food supply was quickly **depleted**, a *trip to the store was necessary to get additional supplies.*

   Synonyms: diminish, drain

   Antonym: enrich

3. **detract**   dǐ-trăkt′   verb

   Etymology: de (down, apart, away) tract (pull)

   To draw or take away; divert

   Be careful not to **detract** *from the main points of the speech with jokes or humorous situations.*

   Synonyms: divert

   Antonyms: enhance, optimize

4. **deactivate**   dē-ăk'tə-vāt'   verb

Etymology: de (down, apart, away) act (act) -ate (to make or cause to be)

To make inactive or not useful

It is important to **deactivate** your security alarm once you enter your home so that the alarm *does not go off* and the police are notified that an intruder might be present in your home.

Synonym: shut down

Antonym: activate

5. **telegraph**   tĕl'ĭ-grăf'   noun/verb

Etymology: tele (from a distance) graph (something written)

(noun) A device used to transmit signals as messages via electronic signals

The use of the Internet has made sending a **telegraph** obsolete because it is much easier and cost effective to *send messages* via email.

(verb) To send by telegraph

In 1844, Samuel Morse **telegraphed** the message—'What God hath wrought' *by wire over a great distance.*

6. **graphology**   gră-fŏl'ə-jē   noun

Etymology: graph (something written) ology (the study of; science of)

The study of handwriting, especially when employed as a means of analyzing character

After studying handwriting for four years, Dectective Smith was named chief of the **Graphology** Department. His *analysis of criminals through their handwriting* helped him solve many cases.

7. **graphic**   grăf'ĭk   adjective

Etymology: graph (something written) ic (relating to or pertaining to)

Giving a lot of detail so that you have a clear idea of something

The witness's **graphic** *details of the murder scene* caused everyone to gasp in surprise.

Synonym: vivid

Antonym: vague

Practice Exercises

MULTIPLE CHOICE

1. Which of the following would <u>decline</u>?
   a. your grade point average if you do not study
   b. the money in your checkbook as your paycheck is deposited
   c. the average age of freshmen if more nontraditional students enrolled
   d. the number of car accidents on a rainy night

2. Which of the following could be <u>depleted</u>?
   a. the number of students who are on the dean's list
   b. natural resources in our country
   c. a new style of living room furniture
   d. a plaid wool skirt

3. What does it mean if your work history <u>detracts</u> from your ability to get a job?
   a. You are very employable and can have your pick of jobs.
   b. You have experience in the type of job you are seeking.
   c. You do not have enough of the right type of experience.
   d. You have excellent references.

4. Why would you want to <u>deactivate</u> something?
   a. to make it work better
   b. to make it stop working
   c. to make it work faster
   d. to share it with your friends

5. What would you send by <u>telegraph</u>?
   a. a long love letter
   b. a short important message
   c. your mother's cookie recipe
   d. an online essay exam answer

6. If you were a student of <u>graphology</u>, which of the following would you look at?
   a. a handwritten postscript to a letter
   b. fingerprints
   c. someone's facial expressions
   d. someone's reaction time in a traffic accident

7. What would you expect to see in a <u>graphic</u> novel?
   a. pictures
   b. illustrations
   c. few words
   d. all of the above

FILL IN THE BLANK   Select the BEST word for each sentence. Use each word only once.

declined	detracts	depleted	deactivated
telegraphed	graphology	graphically	

1. Buying a new house and new furniture _____ the couple's saving account; therefore, they struggled to pay their monthly bills.

2. Jim _____ the connection on his computer to the Internet so his son would not be able to go on the Internet while Jim was away.

3. The artist _____ illustrated the mood of the scene without using any words.

4. The television show was canceled when the number of viewers _____ from 72% of the audience to 15%.

5. The troops that were hidden behind the enemy lines _____ a coded message with their location to headquarters.

6. When you are writing a report, use white paper and plain print so that nothing _____ from the information.

7. Comparing how two people write the same word is an example of _____.

CORRECT OR INCORRECT?   If the sentence is correct, write a "C" on the line provided. If not, write an "I" for incorrect, then REWRITE the sentence to make it correct. You can change any part of the sentence to make it correct.

1. Because of the <u>decline</u> in sales, the store's profits drastically improved.

_____

2. Jack called the phone company to <u>deactivate</u> "caller ID" on his phone because he wanted to be able to see who was calling.

———————————————————————————————————

3. I tried to <u>telegraph</u> Joe the multiple choice answers by tapping on the desk with my pencil.

———————————————————————————————————

4. Every month I put some money into my savings account. It makes me feel good to watch my money <u>deplete</u>.

———————————————————————————————————

5. I thought her wild earrings <u>detracted</u> from her elegant evening gown.

———————————————————————————————————

6. In order to identify the stolen car, the police brought in an expert in <u>graphology</u> to examine the ID number and odometer.

———————————————————————————————————

7. Julie <u>graphically</u> described the landscape so well that Sam could practically see it in his mind.

———————————————————————————————————

SHORT ANSWER   Write your answers on a separate sheet of paper.

1. Name two types of invitations you would <u>decline</u>. Explain your answer.

2. Think about the appliances and electronic equipment you regularly use. What are some things that could be <u>deactivated</u>? Think of at least three.

3. Make a concept map with *graph* at the center and <u>telegraph</u>, <u>graphology</u>, and <u>graphic</u> as three spokes. Add the definitions and other words you know with the same root.

4. What would be the problem if we <u>depleted</u> our water supply?

5. What are two things that would <u>detract</u> from your understanding of a professor's lecture?

6. What are two ads in magazines or on TV that <u>graphically</u> get their point across without using many words?

Power Words

1. **surpass**   sər-păs′   verb

   To be or go beyond, as in degree or quality; exceed

   After studying for three weeks for her calculus test, she was pleasantly surprised with a perfect paper—she **surpassed** *even her highest expectations.*

   Synonyms: exceed, excel

2. **poise**   poiz   verb

   To be balanced or held in suspension

   The alligator *stopped* and **poised** *before he attacked.*

   poise   poiz   noun

   A state of balance or equilibrium; stability

   Mary was praised for her work at the Customer Complaint Counter because of her **poise** *and tact* when talking with angry customers.

   Synonyms: (verb) position, stabilize; (noun) dignity, composure

3. **inhale**   ĭn-hāl′   verb

(Note alternate meaning of *in-*: into)

To draw into the lungs by breathing

While in the doctor's office, Alyssa was told to **inhale** deeply so that the doctor could assess her lung capacity.

To consume rapidly or eagerly; devour

A.J. **inhaled** his first meal *after being stranded without food for three days* on the desert island.

Synonyms: breathe, devour

Practice Exercises

1. Describe a time when you <u>surpassed</u> your own expectations.

2. How would someone with <u>poise</u> act if they dropped a tray full of food in the cafeteria?

3. Name two things that are dangerous to <u>inhale</u>.

Chapter Review

Yes or No?

Read the sentence and answer the questions.

1. Bob's heartbeat was <u>irregular</u> and his medical tests <u>inconsistent</u> with what is considered healthy.

    a. Was Bob's heartbeat normal? _____

    b. Were the results of his medical tests different from normal? _____

    c. Was Bob in good health? _____

2. There was insurmountable evidence that the treasurer had committed <u>illegal</u> acts and had <u>depleted</u> the company's savings.

    a. Did the treasurer break the law? _____

    b. Did the treasurer put more money into the savings? _____

3. Joseph kept his <u>poise</u> even though he was <u>infuriated</u> at the <u>improper</u> service he received in the restaurant.

    a. Did Joseph lose his temper? _____

    b. Was Joseph happy with the service he got at the restaurant? _____

    c. Did Joseph get good service at the restaurant? _____

Expanded Word Forms

infuriate   infuriating   infuriated   deactivate   deactivated
decline   declining   declined   deactivation

1. Drivers who drive below the speed limit _____ me.

2. Billy _____ his mother when he smeared grape jelly on the wall.

3. It is _____ to have to wait for hours in the doctor's office.

4. Sue _____ Bob's marriage proposal because she had only known him for one week. He knew she would probably _____ the proposal, but he wanted her to know how much he loved her. While _____, Sue was careful to let Bob know she still wanted to date him.

5. In order to reset our cable box, we had to _____ the connection to the television. The _____ took only a few minutes. After we had _____ the box and restarted it, we were able to watch the shows we wanted.

Expand Your Learning

You learned in Chapter One that it is important to use a variety of strategies when learning and reviewing material. Do one or more of the following exercises to practice the words in this chapter.

Using your vision and color:

1. Write the words on note cards. Put the word on the front and the definition on the back. Use a different-color ink for the different categories of words according to the various word parts. To review the words, you should use three steps.
   a. Pronounce the word on the front.
   b. Try to remember the definition in your own words.
   c. Look at the back to check your answer.

   Separate the words into two piles, the ones you know and the ones you missed. Keep reviewing the ones you missed until you can recite them all correctly. You should repeat this several times during the week. Be sure to mix up the cards so you do not always do them in the same order.

2. Group the words according to their different word parts. Write each group in a different-color ink. Outline the shape of each word.

3. Draw simple stick figures to illustrate the meaning of each word.

4. Go back to the Fill in the Blank exercises and underline the context clues in each sentence that helped you identify the correct word.

5. Find other words that use the word parts in this chapter. Keep a list of words with each word part and add to it as you find more words throughout the semester.

Using your voice and hearing:

1. Make note cards as explained in the preceding exercise using vision. You do not need to use different-color inks unless you want to. When you go through the cards, say the words and the definitions out loud.

2. Go back to the Fill in the Blank exercises and read the sentences out loud. This would be a good way for you to check that you have used each word correctly.

Using large and small muscles:

1. Fold a piece of paper in half lengthwise and label the columns A and B. Write the words in column A and the definitions in B. Fold back column A and recite the words from the definitions; then do the reverse. Review the words as you do some sort of physical activity such as walking or riding an exercise bike.

2. Put the words and definitions on note cards as explained in the preceding exercise using vision. You do not need to use different-color inks unless you want to. Carry these cards with you and review them throughout the day as you do your daily activities such as brushing your teeth, eating breakfast, etc.

Puzzle Fun

Each hint is an _antonym_ for a vocabulary word. Read the hint; find the vocabulary word.

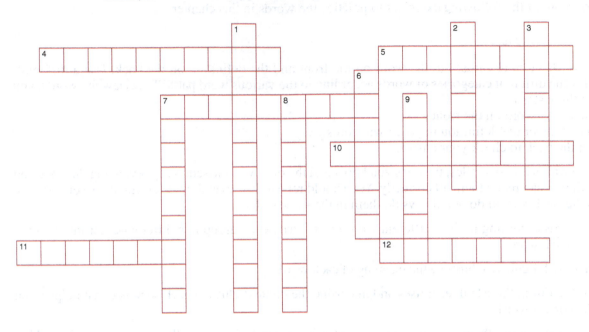

Across

4. necessary
5. fitting
7. coherent
10. activate
11. good
12. optimize

Down

1. unchanging
2. vague
3. enrich
6. lawful
7. consistent
8. to please
9. accept

CHAPTER FIVE

More Context Clues

The limits of my language are the limits of my mind.
All I know is what I have words for.

Ludwig Wittgenstein, philosopher (1889–1951)

CHAPTER OBJECTIVE

Students will be able to identify and use words with the following common structural elements:

Prefixes: mono-, uni-, bi-, di-, tri-, quad-, penta-, pro-, retro-
Suffixes: -(o)logy, -ist, -ian

CHAPTER OUTLINE

 Memory Tip   Overlearn the Material

 Vocabulary Strategy   Context Clues Part II

Part A
Words to Learn

monopoly	trilogy
unilateral	quadruple
bilateral	pentagon
dilemma	

Structural Elements

mono-,	uni-
bi-, di-	tri-
quad-	penta-

Part B
Words to Learn

gerontology	gerontologist
theology	theologian
archaeology	archaeologist
provoke	retroactive
proactive	retrospect

Structural Elements

-(o)logy	-ian,	-ist
pro-		
retro-		

Power Words

abide	adage	abdicate

***Memory Tip*   Overlearn the Material**

There is a big difference between studying to the point of *recognition* compared to the point of *recall*. Don't think you will *recognize* the correct answer when you see it on the exam—this rarely works. Instead, study to the point where you can *recall* the information from your memory with little or no prompting. Then study it one more time to the point of overlearning.

 ***Vocabulary Strategy*   Context Clues Part II**

In Chapter Four you were introduced to context clues. The final two types of context clues are:

- contrast/antonyms

- cause and effect

In some sentences you may find context clues of *contrast/antonymns*. In this case the author adds words to tell you what the unknown word is not. Examples of signals to this type of clue are:

- *but*

- *even though*

- *yet*

- *however*

- *although*

- *on the other hand*

- *conversely*

- *on the contrary*

- *despite*

Cause and effect context clues illustrate the relationship between sentences or clauses. The "what happened/effect" and "why did it happen/cause" are signaled by words such as:

- *because/because of*

- *due to*

- *in order to/in order that*

- *since*

- *so, so that*

- *therefore*

- *as a result*

- *consequently*

Part A

WORDS TO LEARN—SEE AND SAY   Use the pronunciation guide on the first page of this book to help you SAY each word.

1.	monopoly	mə-nŏp'ə-lē
2.	unilateral	yōō'nə-lăt'ər-əl
3.	bilateral	bī-lăt'ər-əl
4.	dilemma	dĭ-lĕm'ə
5.	trilogy	trĭl'ə-jē

6. quadruple   kwŏ-drōō′pəl

7. pentagon   pĕn′tə-gŏn′

 STRUCTURAL ELEMENTS   Look at the structural elements of each word. Use these elements to unlock the word's meaning.

mono-, uni-	one
bi-, di-	two
tri-	three
quad-	four
penta-	five

 CONTEXT CLUES   Read the sentences. Use the words around the unfamiliar word to determine the word's meaning. Words in bold are the vocabulary words; words in italic are the context clues.

1. After three months of testimony, the judge ruled that the company had *exclusive control;* therefore, it was guilty of violating the **monopoly** laws.

2. Many CEOs feel that the decision-making process in their companies should be **unilateral** with little or *no input from the employees* concerning vacations, raises, etc.

3. At Cherry Creek Academy the students had to come up with a **bilateral** agreement that would benefit *both the female and male* students involved. The result was an activities calendar that included sports, formal events, and concerts.

4. When faced with a **dilemma,** it is helpful to list all consequences for the *two possible positions* before making a decision.

5. Alyssa, Mia, and Emily each chose one of the *three books* in the **trilogy** for their class book report.

6. Victor **quadrupled** the amount of money that he put into his savings account since he got a new job. Instead of saving $25 a week, he is saving *four times as much,* or $100.

7. The new bride chose **pentagon**-shaped china; each plate had *five sides* as opposed to being circular.

 DICTIONARY   Read the following definitions.

1. **monopoly**   mə-nŏp′ə-lē   noun

   Etymology: mono (one) poly (many)

   Exclusive control by one group

   The government will investigate any charge that a company is a **monopoly;** that is, a company that has *total control* of a product.

   Synonym: dominance

2. **unilateral**   yōō′nə-lăt′ər-əl   adjective

   Etymology: uni (one) lateral (side)

   Relating to, involving, or affecting only one side

   The students argued that the university's decision to dissolve the fraternity was **unilateral** because they, the students, *did not have any input.*

3. **bilateral**   bī-lăt′ər-əl   adjective

   Etymology: bi (two) lateral (side)

   Having or formed of two sides

A **bilateral** ruling was made by the Senate; *both Republicans and Democrats* agreed with the new law.

Synonyms: reciprocal, respective

4. **dilemma**   dĭ-lĕm'ə   noun

   Etymology: di (two) lema (premise, anything received or taken)

   A problem that presents two undesirable alternatives

   A.J. worked for the lumber company for only three weeks when he was faced with the **dilemma** *between working 50-hour weeks and being unemployed.*

   Vocabulary Tip: The dictionary definition for *dilemma* refers to a situation in which a choice must be made between two courses of action or argument. However, common usage of the term simply means "a problem" or "a predicament."

   Synonyms: difficulty, crisis

5. **trilogy**   trĭl'ə-jē   noun

   Etymology: tri (three) logy (story)

   A group of three dramatic or literary works related in subject or theme

   The book club enjoyed reading the **trilogy** because the *three books together* gave the story from three different perspectives.

   Synonyms: threesome, triad

6. **quadruple**   kwŏ-drōō'pəl   adjective/verb

   Etymology: quad (four) quadrae (plus)

   (adjective) Consisting of four parts or members

   The four siblings were a **quadruple** terror when left with a babysitter; they were *four times* as difficult to handle than when each child was alone.

   Verb: to make four times greater

   It was necessary to **quadruple** the recipe because *four families were invited to dinner.*

7. **pentagon**   pĕn'tə-gŏn'   noun

   Etymology: penta (five) gon (angles)

   A polygon having five sides and five interior angles

   The geometric shape was a **pentagon**, *that is, a five-sided shape.*

Practice Exercises

MULTIPLE CHOICE

1. How many companies would be involved in a <u>monopoly</u>?
   a. one
   b. two
   c. three
   d. four

2. In a <u>unilateral</u> decision, how many parties make the final decision?
   a. one
   b. two
   c. three
   d. four

3. Why would a <u>bilateral</u> decision be fair to both sides?
   a. One side would have more power than the other.
   b. Three or more parties would make the decision.

    c. Both sides would share equally in the decision.

    d. One side would give in to the demands of the other.

4. Why might you seek advice for a <u>dilemma</u>?
   a. You want to appear smart.
   b. You want help making a decision.
   c. You want to show that you have all the answers.
   d. You want to share your opinion with others.

5. How many parts are in a <u>trilogy</u>?
   a. one
   b. two
   c. three
   d. four

6. Which of the following numbers is <u>quadruple</u> the number 3?
   a. 9
   b. 12
   c. 15
   d. 333

7. How many sides and angles are there on a <u>pentagon</u>?
   a. five sides and four angles
   b. three sides and five angles
   c. six sides and six angles
   d. five sides and five angles

FILL IN THE BLANK   Select the BEST word for each sentence. Use each word only once.

monopoly	unilateral	bilateral	dilemma
quadruple	pentagon	trilogy	

1. Because the Widget Company was the only company that made widgets, it had a _____ and could charge whatever it wanted for its product.

2. The author finished writing the _____. Each book focused on one of the three branches of U.S. government and gave a detailed description of its responsibilities to the country.

3. The baseball player was a _____ threat; he could throw, bat, field, and run.

4. The engagement was a _____ decision; both the prospective bride and groom wanted to get married.

5. When my daughter cleaned her room, it was a _____ decision. I was the only one who cared and wanted to make a change.

6. The _____ I had was to get a root canal or lose my tooth.

7. Tim built a _____-shaped table so each of his five children could have his or her own side.

CORRECT OR INCORRECT?   If the sentence is correct, write a "C" on the line provided. If not, write an "I" for incorrect, then REWRITE the sentence to make it correct. You can change any part of the sentence to make it correct.

1. The divorce was messy; both sides had to make some changes in their demands before they could reach a <u>unilateral</u> decision.

2. The exclusive jewelry was sold in three uptown stores; therefore, each store had a <u>monopoly</u>.

_____

3. Mary knew exactly what to do, so she discussed her <u>dilemma</u> with her therapist.

_____

4. The professors and the administration reached a <u>bilateral</u> decision that pleased both sides.

_____

5. The new movie was the fourth part in the <u>trilogy</u>.

_____

6. My grocery bills <u>quadrupled</u> when my sister and her two children came to live with me.

_____

7. The <u>Pentagon</u> in Washington, D.C., is a five-sided building.

_____

SHORT ANSWER   Write your answers on a separate sheet of paper.

1. Is a stop sign a <u>pentagon</u>? Why or why not?

2. <u>Quadruple</u> the number of *X*s shown here: X X.

3. Why would it be beneficial for a company to have a <u>monopoly</u> when it is selling a product?

4. How many people are involved in a <u>unilateral</u> decision? Give an example of this type of decision.

5. How many people are involved in a <u>bilateral</u> decision? Give an example of this type of decision.

6. Describe a <u>dilemma</u> you or a friend has had in the past year.

7. What is the defining characteristic of a <u>trilogy</u>?

Part B

WORDS TO LEARN—SEE AND SAY   Use the pronunciation guide on the first page of this book to help you SAY each word.

1. gerontology	jĕr'ən-tŏl'ə-jē	gerontologist	jĕr'ən-tŏl'ə-jĭst
2. archaeology	är'kē-ŏl'ə-jē	archaeologist	är'kē-ŏl'ə-jĭst
3. theology	thē-ŏl'ə-jē	theologian	thē-ŏl'ə-jē-n
4. provoke	prə-vōk'		
5. proactive	prō-ăk'tĭv		
6. retroactive	rĕt'rō-ăk'tĭv		
7. retrospect	rĕt'rə-spĕkt'		

STRUCTURAL ELEMENTS   Look at the structural elements of each word. Use these elements to unlock the word's meaning.

-(o)logy	study of
-ian	person who; one that
-ist	person who; one that
pro-	forward
retro-	back

CONTEXT CLUES   Read the sentences. Use the words around the unfamiliar word to determine the word's meaning. Words in bold are the vocabulary words; words in italic are the context clues.

1. A modern branch of science is **gerontology,** *the study of the aged. A person who* specializes in studying the older adult is a **gerontologist.**

2. Her desire to study **archaeology** began when she found *arrowheads and pottery shards* and continued until *she graduated with a degree* as an **archaeologist** in 1999.

3. **Theology** is guided by inspiration and an innate desire to *understand God.* A **theologian**'s responsibility is to help people *understand religion.*

4. Miles **provoked,** *angered,* his mother when he continued to jump in the mud after she asked him to stop.

5. Dale was very **proactive** about keeping gas in his car. He always *planned ahead* and looked for a gas station when there was a quarter of a tank left.

6. The tax law was **retroactive**. You have to pay taxes on money earned *before the tax law was passed.*

7. In **retrospec**t, *looking back on the situation*, I wish I had reacted differently.

 DICTIONARY   Read the following definitions

1. **gerontology**   jĕr'ən-tŏl'ə-jē   noun

   Etymology: gero (grow old) ology (study of)

   The scientific study of the biological, psychological, and sociological phenomena associated with old age and aging

   With the *proliferation of older adults* in the United States, it is necessary for more people to study **gerontology.**

   gerontologist   jĕr'ən-tŏl'ə-jĭst   noun

   A person who studies the biology, psychology, and sociology of the aged

   Maria studied biology and then, after seeing the health care needs of her elderly parents, decided to become a **gerontologist**

   Etymology of: -ist (someone who)

2. **archaeology**   är'kē-ŏl'ə-jē   noun

   Etymology: archeo (ancient) ology (study of)

   The systematic study of past human life and culture by the recovery and examination of evidence, such as graves, buildings, tools, and pottery

   Since Jennifer studied history she decided to get an advanced degree in **archaeology**. Her passion for revealing the *hidden history by examining old artifacts* made her an excellent student.

   Synonym: ancient culture

   archaeologist   är'kē-ŏl'ə-jĭst   noun

   One who is an expert in the study of past human life and culture

   The **archaeologist** uncovered part of the *ancient burial grounds* of the Iroquois tribe in his backyard.

   Etymology of: -ist (someone who)

3. **theology**   thē-ŏl'ə-jē   noun

   Etymology: theo (God or religion) ology (study of)

   The study of the nature of God and religious truth

   Max *studies* **theology** at the *Presbyterian seminary.*

   Synonym: belief

theologian thē-ŏl′ə-jē-n noun

One who studies religion

Since he became a **theologian,** he sees the world in a more philosophical way—his *spiritual understanding* helps him to deal with problems that would otherwise control him.

Etymology of: -ian (person that)

4. **provoke** prə-vōk′ verb

Etymology: pro (forward, forth) vok (to call)

To incite to anger or resentment; to bring about a strong reaction

You can **provoke** that lion if you want, but if he *responds by attacking*, don't come running to me for help.

Synonyms: stimulate, challenge, anger, annoy

Antonyms: delight, please

5. **proactive** prō-ăk′tĭv adjective

Etymology: pro (forward, forth) act

Acting in advance to deal with an expected difficulty

Company Elite has taken several **proactive** measures to make sure that it *stays ahead* of the competition in sales.

Synonym: active

Antonym: passive

Vocabulary Tip: If you break down the word *proactive*, it's easy to understand its meaning. *Pro-* is a Latin prefix that means "forward." When you couple *pro-* with *active*, *proactive* means you are being active about the future. The related word, *retroactive*, refers to something that happens as a reaction to an earlier event.

6. **retroactive** rĕt′rō-ăk′tĭv adjective

Etymology: retro (back) act

Refers to something happening now that affects the past

A **retroactive** tax is one that is passed at one time, but *payable back to a time before* the tax was passed.

7. **retrospect** rĕt′rə-spĕkt′ noun/verb

Etymology: retro (back) spect (see or view)

(noun) Contemplation of things in the past

In **retrospect**—*that is, looking back and comtemplating the past*—we sometimes find ourselves wishing that we had done certain things differently.

(verb) To contemplate the past; to refer back

While **retrospecting** over the events that happened last week, Jim *remembered* several details that gave him a completely new interpretation of everyone's reactions.

Synonyms: (noun) hindsignt; (verb) remember, recall

Anyonym: (noun) forethought

Practice Exercises

MULTIPLE CHOICE

1. Which age group would a <u>gerontologist</u> work with?
    a. 19 years and younger
    b. 20–35 years

    c. 36–50 years

    d. 55 years and older

2. Which of the following would be a name of a <u>theology</u> course?

    a. Ancient Greece 101

    b. The History of Rocks 151

    c. The Study of Human Behavior 210

    d. World Religions 230

3. An <u>archaeologist</u> could help you find out

    a. whether Native Americans lived in your area and how long ago

    b. whether the behavior of your boyfriend is normal or abnormal

    c. why bad things happen to good people

    d. the number of species of animals in your area

4. Which of the following would be a reaction if you were <u>provoked</u>?

    a. "I wish you would stop doing that! You are infuriating me!"

    b. "Congratuations on a job well done!"

    c. "Happy Birthday!"

    d. "Let's see if we can come to a logical next step to solve the problem."

5. Which of the following describes something <u>proactive</u>?

    a. looking back and writing a postscript to the letter

    b. predicting what will happen and taking action to prevent it

    c. having quick reactions to what is happening right now

    d. doing nothing

6. If you take <u>retroactive</u> action you

    a. predict the future

    b. do something illegal and immoral

    c. think about a mistake you made yesterday and fix it now

    d. react immediately to what is happening right now

7. If your mother was thinking in <u>retrospect</u>, what would she say?

    a. "Let's go shopping tomorrow."

    b. "What would you like for dinner?"

    c. "Let's make plans for a family vacation next summer."

    d. "You were so cute when you were a baby."

FILL IN THE BLANK   Select the BEST word for each sentence. Use each word only once.

gerontology/gerontologist   theology/theologian   retroactive   retrospect
archaeology/archaeologist   provoke   proactive

1. The minister at my church has written many books and is a famous _____.

2. Dr. Black majored in _____. All of her patients were senior citizens.

3. In _____, I think we should have acted differently after the accident yesterday.

4. I hope to take a(n) _____ class because I have heard that the students go out into the fields around the campus and look for arrowheads.

5. Carol was very _____ and always looked ahead to see when her exams were scheduled for the next month.

6. I think it is unfair that the new major requirements are _____. I am almost ready to graduate and now I have to take more courses that have been added to my previous course of study.

7. Please don't _____ my new dog. He is not trained yet and may bite if you annoy him.

CORRECT OR INCORRECT? If the sentence is correct, write a "C" on the line provided. If not, write an "I" for incorrect, then REWRITE the sentence to make it correct. You can change any part of the sentence to make it correct.

1. I took our new baby to the <u>gerontologist</u> to get his vaccinations.

   _____

2. Sam consulted the local <u>theologian</u> to try to understand why his wife shopped so much and spent so much money.

   _____

3. The museum had an <u>archaeologist</u> on staff to determine the age of the ancient fabric.

   _____

4. Joey was very <u>proactive</u> and laid back and never worried about the future.

   _____

5. I am very <u>provoked</u> by all of the spam messages that are clogging my email.

   _____

6. When Dr. Homes <u>retroactively</u> raised all of the students' grades, it raised my grade point average so much that I was on the Dean's List.

   _____

7. I enjoy moments of <u>retrospection</u>, thinking about what I am going to do in the future.

   _____

SHORT ANSWER Write your answers on a separate sheet of paper.

1. Why would it be difficult to be a <u>gerontologist</u>?
2. Why would you go to see a <u>theologian</u>?
3. What would an <u>archaeologist</u> tell you about pottery fragments found on a Native American Indian reservation?
4. If you were being <u>proactive</u>, what would you do regarding your college courses?
5. Name three things that <u>provoke</u> you.
6. If you were able to make a <u>retroactive</u> change, what one change would you make?
7. When you have time for <u>retrospection</u>, what is one event in your life that you like to think about?

Power Words

1. **abide**   ə-bīd′   verb

   To conform to

   It is necessary to **abide** by, *or follow*, the laws if you don't want to get into trouble.

   To put up with; tolerate

   Because she is an optimist, Sue cannot **abide** people who complain all the time and *tries not to socialize with them.*

   Synonyms: accept, acknowledge

2. <u>adage</u>   ăd′ĭj   noun

   A saying that sets forth a general truth and that has gained credit through long use

   A familiar **adage** is "*A stitch in time saves nine.*"

   Synonyms: proverb, axiom

3. <u>abdicate</u>   ab′dĭ-kāt′   verb

   To relinquish power formally; to give up a position

   The CEO of Xtrema **abdicated** his position and *retired* after he found out that he had major health problems.

   Synonym: resign

Practice Exercises

1. Name two things you cannot <u>abide</u>.

2. What is your favorite <u>adage</u>? Explain its meaning. (Hint: This might be something your parents told you many times when you were a small child.)

3. Name two positive reasons and two negative reasons why a person in power (either government or business) might <u>abdicate</u> his or her position.

Chapter Review
Related Words with Prefixes

Make a seven-column chart and head each column with a prefix from Part A of this chapter. Using a dictionary and from your reading, compile more words that have the same prefix. Write the definition in the column with each new word.

Related Words with Suffixes

Make a chart with two columns, one labeled *-(o)logy* and one labeled *-ian, -ist*. Using your dictionary or any other source, list words and their meanings in the two columns. You can also make up your own words, for example:

-(o)logy	*-ian, -ist*
nonsenseology—*the study of nonsense*	nonsensian—*someone who studies nonsense*

Expanded Word Forms

retrospect	retrospectively	provoke	provoked	provoking	
monopoly	monopolize	quadruples	quadrupled	proactive	proactively

1. Do not _____ the conversation. Let someone else have a chance to speak.

2. The furniture store had a _____ in the town. No other store sold chairs and couches.

3. When they are out of season, the price of strawberries usually _____.

4. To train for the marathon last year, Jack _____ the number of miles that he ran each day.

5. Joyce was very _____, she always looked ahead to see how to prepare for her classes. She found that working _____ helped her to always be prepared for classes and exams.

6. In _____, I think you should have said something different when Sally asked you whether you liked her new haircut. Thinking _____ helps you to understand what happened and to act differently in the future.

7. I find it very _____ when me friend lets her new dog jump all over me. I am surprised she does not think the dog's actions would _____ me. Even though the dog's actions _____ me in the past, my friend still lets her dog jump on me every time we meet.

Expand Your Learning

You learned in Chapter One that it is important to use a variety of strategies when learning and reviewing material. Do one or more of the following exercises to practice the words in this chapter.

Using your vision and color:

1. Write the words on note cards. Put the word on the front and the definition on the back. Use a different-color ink for the different categories of words according to the various word parts. To review the words, you should use three steps.
   a. Pronounce the word on the front.
   b. Try to remember the definition in your own words.
   c. Look at the back to check your answer.

   Separate the words into two piles, the ones you know and the ones you missed. Keep reviewing the ones you missed until you can recite them all correctly. You should repeat this several times during the week. Be sure to mix up the cards so you do not always do them in the same order.

2. Group the words according to their different word parts. Write each group in a different-color ink. Outline the shape of each word.

3. Draw simple stick figures to illustrate the meaning of each word.

4. Go back to the Fill in the Blank exercises and underline the context clues in each sentence that helped you identify the correct word.

5. Find other words that use the word parts in this chapter. Keep a list of words with each word part and add to it as you find more words throughout the semester.

Using your voice and hearing:

1. Make note cards as explained in the preceding exercise using vision. You do not need to use different-color inks unless you want to. When you go through the cards, say the words and the definitions out loud.

2. Go back to the Fill in the Blank exercises and read the sentences out loud. This would be a good way for you to check that you have used each word correctly.

Using large and small muscles:

1. Fold a piece of paper in half lengthwise and label the columns A and B. Write the words in column A and the definitions in B. Fold back column A and recite the words from the definitions; then do the reverse. Review the words as you do some sort of physical activity such as walking or riding an exercise bike.

2. Put the words and definitions on note cards as explained in the preceding exercise using vision. You do not need to use different-color inks unless you want to. Carry these cards with you and review them throughout the day as you do your daily activities such as brushing your teeth, eating breakfast, etc.

Puzzle Fun

Read each sentence. Complete the sentence with a vocabulary word from this chapter. Write the vocabulary word in the crossword puzzle.

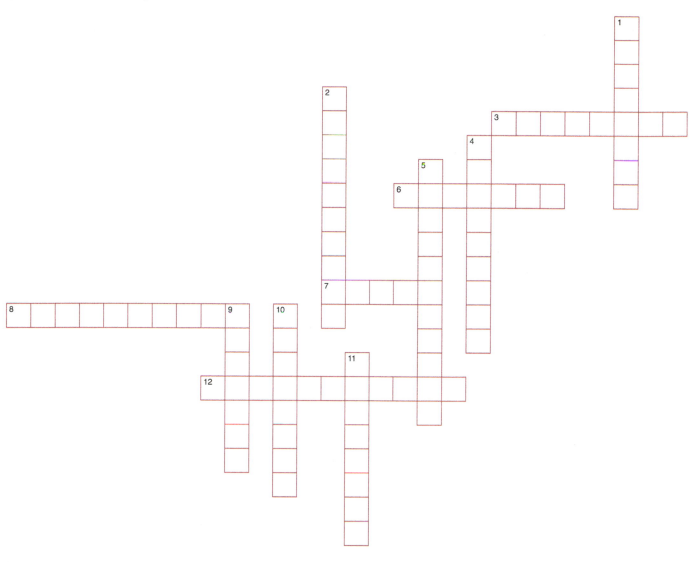

Across

3. The king was asked to _____ the throne after his kingdom was conquered by the enemy.
6. Alyssa, Mia, and Emily each chose one of the three books in the _____ for their class book report.
7. Because she is an optimist, Sue cannot _____ people who complain all the time and tries not to socialize with them.
8. Victor _____ the amount of money that he put into his savings account since he got a new job. Instead of saving $25 a week, he is saving four times as much, or $100.
12. A modern branch of science is _____, the study of the aged.

Down

1. The new bride chose _____-shaped china; each plate had five sides as opposed to being circular.
2. My father felt that the decision-making process in our family should be _____ with little or no input from the rest of us concerning vacations, housing, schooling, etc.
4. At Cherry Creek Academy the students had to come up with a _____ agreement that would benefit both the female and male students involved. The result was an activities calendar that included sports, formal events, and concerts.
5. Her desire to study _____ began when she found arrowheads and pottery shards.
9. When faced with a _____, it is helpful to list all consequences for the two possible positions before making a decision.
10. _____ is guided by inspiration and an innate desire to understand God.
11. After three months of testimony, the judge ruled that the company had exclusive control; therefore, it was guilty of violating the _____ laws.

CHAPTER SIX
The Dictionary as a Tool

Words once spoken can never be recalled.

Wentworth Dillon, English poet (1630–1685)

CHAPTER OBJECTIVE

Students will be able to identify and use words with the following common structural elements:

Prefixes: vi-, viv-, mort-, intra-, inter-, geo-

CHAPTER OUTLINE

 Memory Tip   Memory Techniques: Visualization, Association, Mnemonics

Vocabulary Strategy   Dictionary Use

Part A
Words to Learn

vitality	vivacious
vicarious	mortal
mortician	morgue
mortify	

Part B
Words to Learn

interpersonal	interstate
interim	geology
intramural	geography
intrastate	geocentric

Structural Elements

vi-, viv-	mort-

Structural Elements

intra-	inter-
geo-	

Power Words

verbose	valid
facsimile	

Memory Tip   Memory Techniques: Visualization, Association, Mnemonics

During the beginning stages of learning, there are memory techniques that you can use to learn the material more easily:

1. *Visualization*—Try to picture what you are learning. For example, in this chapter two of the words are *vitality* (having energy) and *vivacious* (lively). To help yourself learn these words you can picture a friend who has these qualities while you work with the words.

2. *Association*—The preceding illustration is also an example of association. You are associating the vocabulary words with something you already know. In any class, if you can associate, or connect, what you are learning with what you already know or experiences you have had, you will have an easier time learning the new information.

3. *Mnemonics*—A mnemonic is a word or phrase that you make up to help with the very beginning of learning. Once you have learned the information you will no longer need the help. A common mnemonic in math is "Please excuse my dear Aunt Sally," or PEMDAS, to help remember the order of operations in solving a complex problem (parentheses, exponents, multiplication, division, addition, subtraction). Expert mathematicians no longer use this, but beginning math students find it invaluable! You can make your own mnemonics by inventing a word or phrase using the first letters in the words or the information you need to learn.

Vocabulary Strategy   Dictionary Use

We can find word meanings in many ways. In this chapter we will review the final step in SSCD—using a dictionary.

The textbook glossary should be the first dictionary consulted when reading a textbook. The glossary defines words as they are used in that specfic discipline.

The Internet provides several dictionaries that give you not only definitions but also pronunciations, the origin or history, and often an audio of the word. Keep in mind that frequently a word will have multiple definitions. In the dictionary the most common definition is listed first. This may not be the exact definition the author is using, so be open to the other definitions for the word you need.

Part A

WORDS TO LEARN—SEE AND SAY   Use the pronunciation guide on the first page of this book to help you SAY each word.

1. vitality   vī-tăl′ĭ-tē
2. vivacious   vĭ-vā′shəs
3. vicarious   vī-kâr′ē-əs
4. mortal   môr′tl
5. mortify   môr′tə-fī′
6. mortician   môr-tĭsh′ən
7. morgue   môrg

 STRUCTURAL ELEMENTS   Look at the structural elements of each word. Use these elements to unlock the word's meaning.

vi-, viv-   life

mort-   death

CONTEXT CLUES   Read the sentences. Use the words around the unfamiliar word to determine the word's meaning. Words in bold are the vocabulary words; words in italic are the context clues.

1. The cheerleader's **vitality** was contagious; her *energy and cheerfulness* made everyone in the stadium want to stand up and cheer.

2. The charming and **vivacious** hostess welcomed each guest with a *big smile* as she handed each a small gift.

3. Although her health prohibited her from participating in any athletic activities, Agnes *watched* the sporting event and *enjoyed the activity* even if it was only a **vicarious** experience.

4. The young boy was an extreme fan of the movie *Superman*; he had a difficult time realizing that he was **mortal** and *capable of dying* if he tried to do the stunts that Superman did.

5. The principal tried to **mortify** the misbehaving group of students. He thought by *embarrassing* them and placing them in the center court of the school with a sign stating, "These students disobeyed school policy," that they would change their behavior.

6. Before you can enter a program of study to become a **mortician**, *or funeral director*, you must have successfully earned six college credits.

7. The emergency **morgue** is located inside city hall. This makes it easier for the *dead bodies* to be assembled for identification.

 DICTIONARY   Read the following definitions.

1. **vitality**   vī-tăl′ĭ-tē   noun

   Etymology: vi (life) -ity (state of being)

   Physical or intellectual vigor; energy

   After months of battling cancer, her **vitality** seemed to be *destroyed* and she *was tired most of the time.*

   Synonym: liveliness

2. **vivacious**   vĭ-vā′shəs   adjective

   Etymology: vi (life) ious (full of or characteristic of)

   Full of animation and spirit; lively

   Alyssa's **vivacious** personality made her the most likely student to win the title "Miss Congeniality."

   Synonym: spirited

3. **vicarious**   vī-kâr′ē-əs   adjective

   Etymology: vi (life) ious (full of or characteristic of)

   Felt or undergone as if one were taking part in the experience or feelings of another

   Many of us have a **vicarious** experience of mountain climbing. We can *watch the climbers and feel their thrill.*

4. **mortal**   môr′tl   noun

   Etymology: mort (death) al (relates to or pertains to)

   A human; capable of dying

   After watching the sci-fi channel, Mia was *confused* because she didn't know who were truly **mortals** and who were *the aliens.*

   mortal   adjective

   Relating to, or accompanying, death

   Breathing is essential for any **mortal** being. *Without it a person would die.*

   Synonyms: (noun) person, being, creature; (adj) terminal

5. **mortify**   môr'tə-fī'   verb

Etymology: mort (death) ify (to make like)

To cause to experience shame, humiliation, or wounded pride; humiliate

A teacher should be careful so as not to **mortify**, or *greatly embarass*, a student who has given an incorrect response.

Synonyms: disgrace, embarrass

6. **mortician**   môr-tĭsh'ən   noun

Etymology: mort (death) ian (someone or something that pertains to)

Funeral director

The **mortician** prepared a demonstration for the students who were interested in becoming a *funeral director.*

Synonym: funeral director

7. **morgue**   môrg   noun

Etymology: mort (dead) gue (house of)

A place in which the bodies of deceased persons are kept until identified and claimed or until arrangements for burial have been made

The high school seniors had a field trip to the **morgue**. After seeing the *dead bodies,* many of the students became ill.

Practice Exercises

MULTIPLE CHOICE

1. Which of the following words describe someone with <u>vitality</u>?
   a. high energy, pep
   b. messy, unorganized
   c. tired, sleepy
   d. embarrassed, uneasy

2. Why would you want to have a friend who is <u>vivacious</u>?
   a. because he or she would say "no" to every activity
   b. because he or she would be easily embarrassed and easy to make fun of
   c. because he or she would be lively and energetic
   d. because you could experience life through him or her

3. How could you have a <u>vicarious</u> experience?
   a. by having a near death experience
   b. by always living life to the fullest and doing everything you want
   c. by being the brunt of a practical joke
   d. by listening to someone else describe what he or she experienced

4. Which of the following are characteristics of those who are <u>mortal</u>?
   a. They will eventually die.
   b. They will live forever.
   c. They are extremely embarrassed.
   d. They work in a funeral home.

5. In which situation might you be <u>mortified</u>?
   a. You work in a funeral home.
   b. You drop your lunch tray in a cafeteria full of people.
   c. You are full of life and have a lot of friends.
   d. You are shy and like to experience things through your friends.

6. Where would a <u>mortician</u> work?
   a. Family Life Center
   b. Center for Positive Living
   c. Cedars Skilled Nursing Facility
   d. Trenz Funeral Home

7. What would you find in a <u>morgue</u>?
   a. newborn babies
   b. senior citizens
   c. dead bodies
   d. teenagers playing pool and basketball

FILL IN THE BLANK   Select the BEST word for each sentence. Use each word only once.

vitality	vivacious	vicarious	
mortal	mortified	mortician	morgue

1. Sam was _____ when he discovered that his date thought he was someone else when she had accepted his invitation to dinner and a movie.

2. The _____ professor's classes were always the first ones filled because the students enjoyed her lively lectures and felt they learned a lot.

3. The new puppy had so much _____ that it never seemed to sleep.

4. I enjoy the _____ experiences I have when I read nonfiction adventure stories.

5. We are all _____, so we should make the most of every day we are alive.

6. Joe was studying to be a _____ so he could take over his father's funeral home.

7. The murder victim was taken to the _____ until the body could be identified.

CORRECT OR INCORRECT?   If the sentence is correct, write a "C" on the line provided. If not, write an "I" for incorrect, then REWRITE the sentence to make it correct. You can change any part of the sentence to make it correct.

1. Jenny had such a joy for life that all her friends were attracted to her because of her <u>mortality</u>.

   _____

2. If I don't get enough sleep, I will not feel <u>vivacious</u>.

   _____

3. His <u>vitality</u> was evidence of his joy for life.

   _____

4. In order for me to learn, I have to experience the information myself, so I learn <u>vicariously</u>.

   _____

5. Arlene was <u>mortified</u> as she stepped on stage and proudly accepted the award for Freshman of the Year.

_____

6. Their healthy newborn daughter was taken to the <u>morgue</u> to be examined by the pediatrician before being taken to her mother's room.

_____

7. The <u>mortician</u> received the body of the murder victim after it was released by the police.

_____

SHORT ANSWER   Write your answers on a separate sheet of paper.

1. Describe the personality of someone who is <u>vivacious</u>.

2. Describe an experience you would prefer to have <u>vicariously</u>.

3. List three ways to increase your <u>vitality</u>.

4. Describe an experience when you were <u>mortified</u>. If you cannot remember one, describe a fictional one.

5. Describe what you think the working hours would be for a <u>mortician</u>.

6. Name one television show in which part of the story takes place in a <u>morgue</u>.

7. Add the prefix *im-* to <u>mortal</u>. What is the meaning of the new word?

Part B

WORDS TO LEARN—SEE AND SAY   Use the pronunciation guide on the first page of this book to help you SAY each word.

1. interpersonal	ĭn′tər-pûr′sə-nəl
2. interim	ĭn′tər-ĭm
3. intramural	ĭn′trə-myŏŏr′əl
4. interstate	ĭn′tər-stāt′
5. intrastate	ĭn′trə-stāt′
6. geology	jē-ŏl′ə-jē
7. geography	jē-ŏg′rə-fē
8. geocentric	jē′ō-sĕn′trĭk

STRUCTURAL ELEMENTS   Look at the structural elements of each word. Use these elements to unlock the word's meaning.

intra-	within; into
inter-	between
geo-	earth

CONTEXT CLUES   Read the sentences. Use the words around the unfamiliar word to determine the word's meaning. Words in bold are the vocabulary words; words in italic are the context clues.

1. Speech is a class that requires that you demonstrate your **interpersonal** communication abilities; that is, your *ability to relate* to your audience.

2. Max looked for a new job for one year; in the **interim** *between jobs* he decided to take online classes at the local community college.

3. *Every member of the class* enjoyed the weekly **intramural** volleyball games.

4. Joe and Jenny had an **interstate** romance; *she lived in one state and he lived in another.*

5. In sixth grade, all of the classes study the **intrastate** historical events, those that happened *within their own state.*

6. Geologist studied the **geology** of the region in order to determine *what existed under the surface of the earth* that caused the frequent earthquakes.

7. Before starting construction on the new amusement park, the developers studied the **geography** of the region to determine the best placement of the rides *in relation to the land* as well as *how many people lived in the area* who would come to the park.

8. The moon *revolves around our earth*, so we are **geocentric** to the moon.

 DICTIONARY   Read the following definitions.

1. **interpersonal**   ĭn′tər-pûr′sə-nəl   adjective

   Etymology: inter (between) person (root word) al (relates to or pertains to)

   Of or relating to the interactions between individuals

   Because she lacked **interpersonal** skills and could not *get along well with others*, she was passed over several times for job promotions.

2. **interim**   ĭn′tər-ĭm   adjective/noun

   Etymology: inter (between) im (that is)

   (adjective) Taking place during an intermediate period of time; temporary

   Because the union did not agree on a contract, both employer and employees decided to develop an **interim** agreement *until the contract was ratified.*

   (noun) An interval of time between one event and another

   The **interim** *between the sequel and the original movie* was three years.

   Synonyms: (adj) acting, provisional; (noun) interval

3. **intramural**   ĭn′trə-myo͞or′əl   adjective

   Etymology: intra (within) al (relates to or pertains to)

   Existing or carried on within the bounds of an institution, especially a school

   Intramural competitions *between teams of students at the university* should be encouraged for everyone.

4. **interstate**   ĭn′tər-stāt′ adjective

   Etymology: inter (between); state (state)

   Going between two or more states

   Joe's territory covered *three states*, so he drove on the **interstate** highways every day.

   Antonym: intrastate

5. **intrastate**   ĭn′trə-stāt′   adjective

   Etymology: intra (within); state (state)

   Relating or existing within the boundaries of the state

   The delivery company specialized in overnight **intrastate** deliveries; they worked only *within their own state.*

   Synonym: statebound

   Antonym: interstate

6. **geology**   jē-ŏl′ə-jē   noun

Etymology: geo (earth) ology (study of)

The study of the origin, history, and structure of the earth

Ever since Angela was very young she was interested in *rock formation;* therefore, when she decided to study **geology,** it came as no surprise.

7. **geography**   jē-ŏg′rə-fē   noun

Etymology: geo (earth) graphy (something written)

The study of the earth and its features; the distribution of life on the earth, including human life; the effects of human activity

The study of **geography** will help you to learn the *climate and the natural resources* in a particular area.

Vocabulary Tip: *Geography* means "description of the earth's surface." It is often confused with a related word, *geology,* which means "study of the earth." Geography is about anything that happens on or above the ground, including how people live and use the land. Geology is the study of the earth's content below the surface, such as rocks and the plates that move causing earthquakes.

8. **geocentric**   jē′ō-sĕn′trĭk   adjective

Etymology: geo (earth) centr (center) ic (relates to)

Relating to the earth's center; having the earth as a center

Before Copernicus's revelation that the universe was sun-centric, people believed that the universe was **geocentric,** *having the earth as the center.*

Practice Exercises

MULTIPLE CHOICE

1. An <u>interpersonal</u> loan is
   a. from the bank to you
   b. from your savings to checking account
   c. from one friend to another
   d. from the government to pay for your tuition

2. Why would an institution need an <u>interim</u> president?
   a. because the previous one retired
   b. because the administrators could not agree when making decisions
   c. because you cannot have too many people in leadership positions
   d. so that there is a definite break in the working of that institution

3. When playing <u>intramural</u> sports, you are competing against
   a. other colleges or universities
   b. the administration and faculty
   c. students who are interested in attending your college or university
   d. other students at your college or university

4. If a truck driver has an <u>interstate</u> license, where can he drive?
   a. completely across the United States
   b. into Canada
   c. only within his home state
   d. into Mexico

5. If a truck driver has an <u>intrastate</u> license, where can she drive?
   a. completely across the United States
   b. into Canda
   c. only within her home state
   d. into Mexico

6. What would you find in a <u>geology</u> lab?
   a. live animal specimens
   b. rocks
   c. maps of the solar system
   d. science fiction novels about the future

7. Which of the following would you study in <u>Geography</u> 101?
   a. land formations such as mountains and rivers
   b. natural resources
   c. climate
   d. all of the above
   e. none of the above

8. A <u>geocentric</u> study of the earth would start where?
   a. at the center of the earth
   b. in your hometown
   c. at the sun—the center of our solar system
   d. the moon

FILL IN THE BLANK   Select the BEST word for each sentence. Use each word only once.

interpersonal	intramural	interim	interstate
intrastate	geology	geography	geocentric

1. The _____ truck driver drove from Ohio to California to deliver his load.

2. The _____ president of the company made many changes that affected how the new president communicates with the stockholders.

3. Geoff became interested in rock formations and fossils after taking a _____ class his freshman year.

4. No matter how smart you are, _____ strengths are an important part of working with other employees and success in business.

5. I enjoy _____ sports at my college, but am not interested in joining a team sponsored by the college.

6. The _____ driver had to transfer his load to another driver at the state line.

7. Joel hired a consultant to study the _____ of the farm he purchased before deciding what crops he should plant and the location for each one.

8. The _____ theory of the universe puts the earth as the center.

CORRECT OR INCORRECT?   If the sentence is correct, write a "C" on the line provided. If not, write an "I" for incorrect, then REWRITE the sentence to make it correct. You can change any part of the sentence to make it correct.

1. The bike race was <u>interstate</u> because at one point the riders crossed the state line.

   _____

2. After an exhaustive search, the company hired an <u>interim</u> president and gave her a ten-year contract.

   _____

3. My company sent me to a workshop to learn <u>interpersonal</u> skills so that I could improve the communication among the employees in my department.

_____

4. For our son's tenth birthday we went on an <u>intrastate</u> tour and visited all the historical spots in our own state.

_____

5. The <u>intramural</u> football squad defeated the team from our neighboring university to win the championship.

_____

6. The mayor wanted to investigate the <u>geology</u> of the region before the path of the new highway was determined.

_____

7. Mary studied the <u>geography</u> of the state she was moving to because she wanted to know what the latest fashions were.

_____

8. The sun is the center of the universe in the <u>geocentric</u> theory.

_____

SHORT ANSWER   Write your answers on a separate sheet of paper.

1. Give an example to show the difference between _inter_<u>personal</u> and _intra_personal.

2. If you could take an <u>interstate</u> trip, where would you go?

3. If you could take an <u>intrastate</u> trip, where would you go?

4. Describe a situation in which a college would hire an <u>interim</u> president.

5. What <u>intramural</u> sports does your college or university offer?

6. Where could you go around your hometown to study the <u>geology</u> of the area?

7. Describe the <u>geography</u> of the area where you live.

8. Take the word <u>geocentric</u> and replace the structural element _geo-_ with another word or structural element to make a new word that describes what is the center of your universe. For example, a movie lover might make the word _moviecentric_.

Power Words

1. **verbose**   vər-bōs′   adjective

   Using or containing an excessive number of words; wordy

   The teacher's **verbose** directions _confused_ even the best students.

   Synonyms: wordy, loquacious

2. **valid**   văl′ĭd   adjective

   Containing ideas from which a conclusion may logically be derived; correctly inferred

   You have a **valid** and _strong_ argument, so I will reconsider my decision.

   Synonyms: authentic, bona fide

3. **facsimile**   făk-sĭm′ə-lē   noun

   An exact copy or reproduction; fax

   You must send a **facsimile**, _or copy_, of your driver's license in order to get a reduced rate on your insurance.

   Synonyms: reproduction, copy

Practice Exercises

1. Write a simple sentence and then rewrite it to make it <u>verbose</u>.

2. What would be a <u>valid</u> argument to cancel final exams?

3. Name two situations in which you would need a <u>facsimile</u> of an original document.

Chapter Review

Concept Maps

Make two concept maps for the words in Part A, one for the words relating to life and one for the words relating to death. Put the prefixes in the middle and words based on those prefixes as the extensions. Using your own reading and knowledge, as well as the dictionary, add more related words to your maps.

Yes or No?

Read the sentence and answer the question.

1. The <u>mortician</u> needed a <u>facsimile</u> of the death certificate issued by the <u>morgue</u>.

   a. Has a body been sent to a funeral home? _____

   b. Was the body examined at an official location? _____

   c. Did the mortician receive a handwritten copy of the certificate? _____

2. The <u>vivacious</u> coed was very <u>verbose</u>, so sometimes professors questioned the <u>validity</u> of her statements.

   a. Was the coed dull and not lively? _____

   b. Did the coed talk a lot? _____

   c. Did the professors listen to and believe what the coed said? _____

3. The <u>interim</u> athletic director canceled all <u>intramural</u> sports.

   a. Was the athletic director hired permanently? _____

   b. Did the director cancel sporting events between neighboring colleges? _____

4. Sue was <u>mortified</u> to dance in public; therefore, she enjoyed herself <u>vicariously</u> at dance recitals.

   a. Did Sue feel comfortable dancing in public? _____

   b. Did Sue ignore the other people dancing at the recitals? _____

Expanded Word Forms

validity	valid	mortal	mortally	mortality
mortify	mortified			

1. Do you have a _____ excuse for missing class? The professor might excuse you after she checks the _____ of your reason.

2. I don't embarrass easily, so it takes a lot to _____ me. But I was _____ when I spilled coffee on the person at the next table in the restaurant.

3. Every one of us is _____.

4. The accident victim was _____ wounded and rushed to the hospital. The _____ rate of people injured in similar accidents is very high.

Expand Your Learning

You learned in Chapter One that it is important to use a variety of strategies when learning and reviewing material. Do one or more of the following exercises to practice the words in this chapter.

Using your vision and color:

1. Write the words on note cards. Put the word on the front and the definition on the back. Use a different-color ink for the different categories of words according to the various word parts. To review the words, you should use three steps.
   a. Pronounce the word on the front.
   b. Try to remember the definition in your own words.
   c. Look at the back to check your answer.

   Separate the words into two piles, the ones you know and the ones you missed. Keep reviewing the ones you missed until you can recite them all correctly. You should repeat this several times during the week. Be sure to mix up the cards so you do not always do them in the same order.

2. Group the words according to their different word parts. Write each group in a different-color ink. Outline the shape of each word.

3. Draw simple stick figures to illustrate the meaning of each word.

4. Go back to the Fill in the Blank exercises and underline the context clues in each sentence that helped you identify the correct word.

5. Find other words that use the word parts in this chapter. Keep a list of words with each word part and add to it as you find more words throughout the semester.

Using your voice and hearing:

1. Make note cards as explained in the preceding exercise using vision. You do not need to use different-color inks unless you want to. When you go through the cards, say the words and the definitions out loud.

2. Go back to the Fill in the Blank exercises and read the sentences out loud. This would be a good way for you to check that you have used each word correctly.

Using large and small muscles:

1. Fold a piece of paper in half lengthwise and label the columns A and B. Write the words in column A and the definitions in B. Fold back column A and recite the words from the definitions; then do the reverse. Review the words as you do some sort of physical activity such as walking or riding an exercise bike.

2. Put the words and definitions on note cards as explained in the preceding exercise using vision. You do not need to use different-color inks unless you want to. Carry these cards with you and review them throughout the day as you do your daily activities such as brushing your teeth, eating breakfast, etc.

Puzzle Fun

Read the definition. Write the BEST vocabulary word in the puzzle.

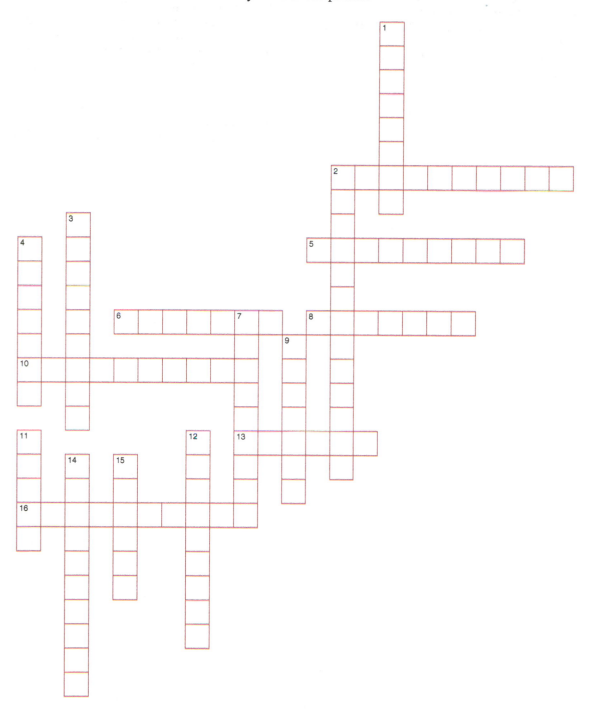

Across

2. existing or carried on within the bounds of an institution, especially a school
5. the study of the earth and its features
6. to cause to experience shame, humiliation, or wounded pride; humiliate
8. using or containing an excessive number of words
10. having the earth as a center
13. relating to, or accompanying, death
16. going between two or more states

Down

1. physical or intellectual vigor
2. of or relating to the interactions between individuals
3. full of animation and spirit
4. the study of the origin, history, and structure of the earth
7. an exact copy or reproduction
9. an interval of time between one event and another
11. correctly inferred
12. felt or undergone as if one were taking part in the experience or feelings of another
14. relating or existing within the boundaries of the state
15. a place in which the bodies of deceased persons are kept until identified and claimed or until arrangements for burial have been made

CHAPTER SEVEN
Words Have Emotions Too

Knowledge speaks, but wisdom listens.

Jimi Hendrix (1942–1970)

CHAPTER OBJECTIVE

Students will be able to identify and use words with the following common structural elements:

Prefixes: e-, ec-, ex-, non-, en-, em-
Suffixes: -tive, -sive, -ive

CHAPTER OUTLINE

 Memory Tip   Space Out Your Learning

 Vocabulary Strategy   Emotional Meaning of Words

Part A
Words to Learn

emit	nonsense
excessive	nondescript
exhale	
exceed	
eccentric	

Structural Elements

e-, ec-, ex-	non-

Part B
Words to Learn

alternative	entrench
objective	enable
passive	engage
empathy	embrace

Structural Elements

-tive, -sive, -ive	en-, em-

Power Words

opaque

translucent

transparent

Memory Tip   Space Out Your Learning

Many students begin marathon study sessions that result in frustration and very little learning. As described in Chapter One, learning requires that studying be spaced out over several sessions.

For your vocabulary, don't do all of the exercises at the same time. At least spread the work of each chapter part, A and B, over two sessions. A separate and final session could then be the Chapter Review and one or more choices from final Expand Your Learning section.

For your other courses, don't try to read a very long chapter or learn massive pages of notes in a single session. Break the material into logical sections (Organize the Material from Chapter Three) and use test/retest to learn each particular portion. Take a break, then move on to the next section.

 ## *Vocabulary Strategy*   Emotional Meaning of Words

One thing that makes language interesting is the fact that many words have an emotional meaning as well as a literal dictionary meaning. These emotional meanings are called connotative meanings, and the literal, or dictionary, meanings are called denotative meanings. For example, would you rather be identified as *skinny* or *thin*? Most people would select *thin* based on its connotative meaning. *Skinny* has the emotional meaning of being unattractive, whereas *thin* would send the message of being in proportion and attractive.

How about *frugal* or *cheap*? Both terms mean "not wanting to spend much money," but which one has a more positive meaning? I am sure that you said *frugal*. *Cheap* has a negative emotional (connotative) meaning, whereas *frugal* indicates something less negative.

Two examples from this book are:

1. See the word <u>antisocial</u> in Chapter 2, Part A. The Vocabulary Tip told you that antisocial implies being disruptive (negative connotation) whereas *unsociable* implies someone who just prefers to be alone.

2. In Chapter 3, Part A the word <u>relevation</u> has the positive connotation of being a pleasant surprise.

Part A

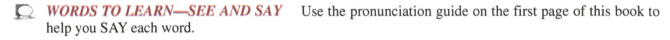 **WORDS TO LEARN—SEE AND SAY**   Use the pronunciation guide on the first page of this book to help you SAY each word.

1. emit   ĭ-mĭt′

2. excessive   ĭk-sĕs′ĭv

3. exhale   ĕks-hāl′

4. exceed   ĭk-sēd′

5. eccentric   ik-sĕn′trĭk

6. nonsense   nŏn′sĕns′

7. nondescript   nŏn′dĭ-skrĭpt′

 STRUCTURAL ELEMENTS   Look at the structural elements of each word. Use these elements to unlock the word's meaning.

e-, ec-, ex-	out
non-	not

 CONTEXT CLUES   Read the sentences. Use the words around the unfamiliar word to determine the word's meaning. Words in bold are the vocabulary words; words in italic are context clues.

1. The sun **emits,** *gives out,* harmful UV rays.

2. The **excessive** heat (*the temperature hit an all-time high* of 101 degrees) caused A.J. to play inside.

3. *After holding her breath* while swimming underwater, Jennifer came to the surface and **exhaled** *before taking another breath.*

4. Don't **exceed** the speed limit. You might get a ticket for *driving over the posted speed.*

5. People consider Megan **eccentric** because she is *so different from all of her friends.*

6. *I can't understand* what you are saying. You are talking **nonsense**.

7. The thief was very **nondescript**. *No one could give any kind of distinguishing characteristics* to help the police.

 DICTIONARY   Read the following definitions.

1. **emit**   ĭ-mĭt′   verb

   Etymology: e (out) mit (send)

   To give out as in sound or matter (commonly light)

   The lamp did not **emit** *enough light* for me to read my book.

   Synonyms: radiate, transmit

2. **excessive**   ĭk-sĕs′ĭv   adjective

   Etymology: ex (out) cess (beyond) ive (to make or cause to be)

   Exceeding a normal or proper limit

   Dr. Jones's students complained about the **excessive** amount of homework that they received each day. Dr. Jones defended his actions by saying that *five pages of algebra problems* was normal when he went to school.

   Synonyms: extreme, exorbitant, extravagant

3. **exhale**   ĕks-hāl′   verb

   Etymology: ex (out) hale (breath)

   To breathe out

   The athletic trainer told his students to make sure that they **exhale,** *or breathe out,* as they are lifting weights.

   Synonym: emit breath

   Antonym: inhale

4. **exceed**   ĭk-sēd′   verb

   Etymology: ex (out) ceed (go or yield)

   To go beyond or outside

   The club was excited to announce that it **exceeded** its expected fund-raising goal by $2,000 *over what it had hoped to raise.*

   Synonym: surpass

   Antonym: fail

   Vocabulary Tip: "*Exceed* and *excess* share the Latin root *excedere* meaning to 'go beyond.' An *excess* is too much of something, like the piles of candy after Halloween, and *exceed* means the action of going too far in a good or bad way." (Vocabulary.com)

5. **eccentric**   ik-sĕn′trĭk   adjective

   Etymology: ec (out) centr (center) ic (relates to)

   Unconventional; not having a common center; odd

The professor's **eccentric**, *uncommon*, mannerisms kept the class amused.

Synonyms: odd, strange, different

Antonym: ordinary

6. **nonsense**   nŏn'sĕns'   noun

    Etymology: non (not) sense

    Words or signs having no intelligible meaning

    The **nonsense** that the judge heard throughout the trial made him doubt the defendant's story because the story had *no logical meaning.*

    Synonym: craziness

    Antonyms: fact, sense

7. **nondescript**   nŏn'dĭ-skrĭpt'   adjective

    Etymology: non (not) descript

    Not having identifying features or qualities

    Often it is better to wear a **nondescript** outfit to a job interview *instead of a flashy one.*

    Synonym: dull

    Antonym: unique

Practice Exercises

MULTIPLE CHOICE

1. Which of the following is an example of <u>emit</u>?
    a. a home run ball
    b. air leaking out of a helium balloon
    c. grass stain on a pair of jeans
    d. finding spelling errors in your homework paper

2. Which of the following would a child like to have in <u>excessive</u> amounts?
    a. homework
    b. candy
    c. dishes to wash and dry
    d. discipline

3. When would you <u>exhale</u>?
    a. when smelling a flower
    b. when tasting a lemon
    c. when blowing out birthday candles
    d. when swallowing milk

4. What happens if your spending <u>exceeds</u> the amount of money in your checking account?
    a. You have enough money in your checking account.
    b. You do not have enough money in your checking account.
    c. Your bank calls to tell you that you have won a prize.
    d. All of the above.

5. Which of the following would describe an <u>eccentric</u> person?
    a. conservative
    b. odd
    c. illogical
    d. immortal

6. Which of the following is <u>nonsense</u>?
   a. Eat your vegetables.
   b. Review your lecture notes after every class.
   c. A penny saved is a penny earned.
   d. Lecture your after review class notes.

7. Which of the following phrases describes a <u>nondescript</u> item?
   a. I want the one with the pink and yellow flowers.
   b. Don't use my favorite mug; it is mine!
   c. Any notebook will do. I don't care what it looks like.
   d. I always buy bright red cars.

FILL IN THE BLANK   Select the BEST word for each sentence. Use each word only once.

emitted   excessive   exhale   exceed
eccentric   nonsense   nondescript

1. The doctor asked Rick to take a deep breath and then _____ so she could check his lungs.

2. Jill didn't realize how _____ she looked when she went to the grocery store in her pajamas.

3. Jimmy was so excited and was talking so fast that his words sounded like _____.

4. The experiment in the chemistry lab _____ such an offensive odor that the entire building had to be evacuated.

5. Tom spent a(n) _____ amount of money on clothes, so he did not have enough to pay for his textbooks.

6. The robber was _____. The witnesses were not able to give the police any clear description.

7. Be careful not to _____ or go over the permitted number of absences in your classes.

CORRECT OR INCORRECT?   If the sentence is correct, write a "C" on the line provided. If not, write an "I" for incorrect, then REWRITE the sentence to make it correct. You can change any part of the sentence to make it correct.

1. Sally was very careful with her money and spent an <u>excessive</u> amount of movies and food.

   _____

2. The toddler <u>emitted</u> a terrible yell whenever her mother left the room.

   _____

3. I love the smell of my mother's chocolate chip cookies, and I took a deep <u>exhale</u> as soon as I walked in the kitchen.

   _____

4. The contestant won the game because she <u>exceeded</u> the time limit for completing the task.

   _____

5. Because of her <u>eccentric</u> behavior and dress, Mary had a hard time making friends at her new school.

   _____

6. My professor's lectures sound like <u>nonsense</u>. He is very organized, speaks slowly, and uses a lot of examples to help the students understand.

   _____

7. Marie's new fur coat was so <u>nondescript</u> that everyone who saw her remembered exactly what the coat looked like.

_____

SHORT ANSWER   Write your answers on a separate sheet of paper.

1. Name two things that might be <u>emitted</u> from a nuclear plant.

2. Name two things that would have a negative effect in <u>excessive</u> amounts. Explain your answer.

3. Name three times when you specifically <u>exhale</u>, not just in your normal breathing.

4. Name three limits you would like to <u>exceed</u>.

5. List three behaviors that would be <u>eccentric</u> at your school. At the local mall.

6. Name three times when what someone says might sound like <u>nonsense</u>.

7. Name two <u>nondescript</u> items you use every day. For example, do you pack your lunch in a <u>nondescript</u> bag you have around the house, or do you have a particular lunch box?

Part B

 WORDS TO LEARN—SEE AND SAY   Use the pronunciation guide on the first page of this book to help you SAY each word.

1.	alternative	ôl-tûr′nə-tĭv
2.	objective	ob-jĕk′tĭv
3.	passive	păs′ĭv
4.	empathy	ĕm′pa-thē
5.	entrench	ĕn-trĕnch′
6.	enable	ĕ-nā′bel
7.	engage	ĕn-gāj′
8.	embrace	ĕm-brās′

 STRUCTURAL ELEMENTS   Look at the structural elements of each word. Use these elements to unlock the word's meaning.

-tive, -sive, -ive	to make or cause to be
en-, em-	in; into

CONTEXT CLUES   Read the sentences. Use the words around the unfamiliar word to determine the word's meaning. Words in bold are the vocabulary words; words in italic are context clues.

1. The **alternative** to _going to the mountains_ would be _to take a trip to my grandmother's house._

2. The **objective,** _or purpose,_ of taking a freshman orientation class is to provide students with an opportunity to experience a broader view of their surroundings.

3. Brandon's **passive** nature caused many people to take advantage of his _easygoing personality._

4. If you are planning on pursuing a career in nursing, it is essential to have **empathy** _for the pain and suffering that many of your patients will be experiencing._

5. After I had my dog for a few weeks, she was so **entrenched** in and _accustomed_ to our daily routine that it upset her if the daily pattern changed.

6. Anne's new job in the admissions office at the community college will **enable**, or *make it possible*, for her to take classes there at no charge.

7. Brenda said that *studying* **engages** *most of her time* now that she is a freshman in college.

8. John **embraced**, *or shared*, his parents' political views only after he researched all of the candidates.

 DICTIONARY   Read the following definitions.

1. **alternative**   ôl-tûr′nə-tĭv   noun

   Etymology: alternate (choice) -ive (to make or cause to be)

   The choice between two mutually exclusive possibilities

   Matthew had to *choose between* going to a community college or the **alternative** of attending a state college in his hometown.

   Synonyms: a substitute, recourse

2. **objective**   ob-jĕk′tĭv   noun/adjective

   Etymology: object (the goal) -ive (to make or cause to be)

   (noun) Something worked toward or striven for; a goal, an intention

   The **objective** of the game is to *get more points than your opponent.*

   (adjective) Uninfluenced by emotions or personal prejudices

   The **objective** critic wrote a *flattering account* of the senior play *even though* he did not like the plot.

   Synonyms: (noun) purpose, target; (adj) fair, unprejudiced

3. **passive**   păs′ĭv   adjective

   Etymology: pass (pass) -ive (to make or cause to be)

   Accepting or submitting without objection or resistance; submissive

   Michael was in sales, and his employer complained that Michael's **passive** attitude was hurting the business because he was *not aggressive enough* when talking to prospective buyers.

   Synonyms: compliant, unassertive

4. **empathy**   ĕm′pa-thē   noun

   Etymology: em (into) pathy (feelings)

   Putting oneself into another's situation, feelings, and motives

   Having **empathy** *for the suffering of others* is a quality that is admired by many.

   Synonyms: understanding, compassion

5. **entrench**   ĕn-trĕnch′   verb

   Etymology: en (into) trench

   To fix firmly or securely; to trespass

   My neighbor's children have slowly become **entrenched** in my yard so that now their toys cover *my yard as well as theirs.*

   Synonyms: anchor, confirm, embed

6. **enable**   ĕ-nā′bel   verb

   Etymology: en (into) able (capable of doing)

To supply with the means, knowledge, or opportunity; make able

The *hole in the fence* **enabled** the dog to *get out of the yard.*

Synonyms: authorize, empower

7. **engage** ĕn-gāj′ verb

Etymology: en (into) gage (pledge)

To draw into; involve

The teacher tried to **engage** the *students in a political discussion* of the problems in the Middle East.

Synonyms: contract, employ, enlist

8. **embrace** ĕm-brās′ verb

Etymology: em (into) brace (the arms)

To clasp or hold with the arms; to welcome; to include

After the long separation, the young soldier and his bride **embraced** *and hugged* for several minutes at his homecoming.

Synonyms: hug, clutch; adopt

Antonym: release

Practice Exercises

MULTIPLE CHOICE

1. Why would you like an <u>alternative</u> for a required class?
   a. in order to choose one that is more interesting
   b. so you do not have to make any decision
   c. so you do not have to think
   d. in order to avoid any substitution

2. What advice would you give a friend who wants to reach an <u>objective</u>?
   a. Sleep on it.
   b. Look for an alternative.
   c. Take a chance.
   d. Work hard.

3. Which of the following is a characteristic of a <u>passive</u> student?
   a. intend to remember
   b. organization
   c. procrastination
   d. time management

4. Which of the following statements would you make if you felt <u>empathy</u> for a friend?
   a. "You infuriate me!"
   b. "I understand how you are feeling."
   c. "I have never felt that way."
   d. "Only people who do not care about their success do that."

5. Which of the following describes someone who is <u>entrenched</u> in her opinion?
   a. someone who finds it very difficult to change
   b. someone who is very flexible and spontaneous
   c. someone who likes to discuss all sides of an issue
   d. someone who always has an open mind

6. Which of the following would <u>enable</u> you to graduate early?
   a. taking as few credits each semester as possible
   b. failing your core courses and having to repeat them
   c. taking summer classes every summer
   d. not listening to your advisor when you register for classes

7. If you are <u>engaged</u> in your work, you are
   a. involved
   b. easily distracted
   c. lost
   d. infuriated

8. Which of the following could you <u>embrace</u>?
   a. your girlfriend or boyfriend
   b. a new puppy
   c. an idea
   d. all of the above

FILL IN THE BLANK   Select the BEST word for each sentence. Use each word only once.

| alternative | objective | passive | embraced |
| empathy | entrenched | enable | engaged |

1. The two convicts were _____ in a power struggle to see who would take control of the cell block.

2. You should not be a(n) _____ learner. It is better to be actively involved.

3. Even though the teacher had great _____, many of her students complained that she just didn't care.

4. The Union Army was _____ in the battlefield; the Confederates could not weaken their lines or get across to the other side.

5. The _____ to calling someone for a ride would be to walk home.

6. I prefer _____ exams instead of ones that ask for my opinion.

7. If I won the lottery, that would _____ me to pay off my college loans and get a new car.

8. When the soldiers returned home, they were _____ by their families as they exited the plane.

CORRECT OR INCORRECT?   If the sentence is correct, write a "C" on the line provided. If not, write an "I" for incorrect, then REWRITE the sentence to make it correct. You can change any part of the sentence to make it correct.

1. Craig was so in love with Sue that she was his <u>alternative</u> choice for a wife.

_____

2. It is helpful to be certain of your <u>objectives</u> when you start a project so you do not do unnecessary work.

_____

3. Gary was a very <u>passive</u> basketball player. He ran all over the court and always tried to get the ball.

_____

4. Emily was able to listen to Lauren's fears about taking tests with <u>empathy</u> even though Emily had never failed an exam.

_____

5. I always felt <u>entrenched</u> in my neighborhood because my family moved every few months.

_____

6. My solid background knowledge in math <u>enabled</u> me to move ahead rapidly in the individualized math course.

_____

7. In order for the car to move forward, the clutch has to be <u>engaged</u>.

_____

8. Tom and Bill were so opposed to the new rules imposed by the council that they <u>embraced</u> the changes willingly.

_____

SHORT ANSWER   Write your answers on a separate sheet of paper.

1. Name two things that are a healthy <u>alternative</u> to soda pop.
2. What is your <u>objective</u> for this class? What is your professor's <u>objective</u> for the class?
3. Describe two things a <u>passive</u> student might do that would get him or her into academic trouble.
4. Describe a situation in which you would have a hard time feeling <u>empathetic</u>.
5. What would you do if a swarm of termites were <u>entrenched</u> in your house?
6. What characteristics do you have that <u>enable</u> you to be a successful college student?
7. Name something that can be <u>engaged</u> besides two people planning to be married.
8. List five people or things that you <u>embrace</u>.

Power Words

1. **opaque** ō-pāk′   adjective

   Not clear; not transmitting light; not able to see through

   The teacher decided to put **opaque** paper on the windows *to eliminate the light.*

   Synonyms: obfuscated, darkened

2. **translucent** trăns-lōō′sent   adjective

   Permitting some light to pass through, but not allowing images to be clearly seen

   Because our front window was level with the sidewalk, we chose **translucent** drapes so that passers-by were *not able to see in clearly.*

   Synonyms: luminous, blurred

3. **transparent** trăns-pâr′ent   adjective

   Capable of transmitting light so that objects or images can be seen; clear

   Her message was very **transparent** *and clear;* she did not like her job and she wanted to quit.

   Because the day care observation room had a **transparent** panel, *parents could observe* their children at work and play.

   Synonym: clear

Practice Exercises

1. Teachers used to use transparencies on an overhead projector. Why are they called <u>transparencies</u>?

2. From the list below, label each as <u>transparent</u>, <u>opaque</u>, or <u>translucent</u>.
   a. ladies' hose
   b. socks
   c. frosted windows
   d. construction paper

e. plastic wrap
f. wax paper
g. water
h. superglue
i. hair gel

Chapter Review

Matching

_____ 1. emit   a. beyond a normal amount

_____ 2. alternative   b. to draw into; involve

_____ 3. excessive   c. to breathe out

_____ 4. opaque   d. without resistance

_____ 5. exhale   e. to give out

_____ 6. objective   f. to fix firmly or securely

_____ 7. passive   g. odd, strange

_____ 8. exceed   h. a choice between two different possibilities

_____ 9. empathy   i. no logical meaning

_____10. translucent   j. understanding how another person feels

_____11. nonsense   k. something to work toward

_____12. transparent   l. letting no light pass through

_____13. entrench   m. to go beyond

_____14. eccentric   n. clear

_____15. enable   o. to supply with the means to do something

_____16. engage   p. permitting some light to pass through

Antonyms (Opposite) and Synonyms (Same Meaning)

Use the words from this chapter to complete the following:

1. _____ is the opposite of *opaque*.

2. _____ is the opposite of *active*.

3. _____ is the opposite of *logic*.

4. _____ is the opposite of *inhale*.

5. _____ is the opposite of *retain*.

6. _____ is the same as *extreme*.

7. _____ is the same as *odd*.

8. _____ is the same as *involve*.

9. _____ is the same as *embedded*.

10. _____ is the same as *compassion*.

Expanded Word Forms

engaging	engaged	engagement	objective	objectively
embrace	embraceable	exhaling	exhale	exhalations

1. "_____ me, my sweet _____ you." (Ira Gershwin 1930)

2. In yoga you practice your breathing, _____ and inhaling. In one exercise you make your _____ slightly longer than your inhale. Your _____ are to be through your nose.

3. Rose has a very _____ personality. All who meet her like to talk with her. She is always _____ in a conversation with someone she has just met. But at Rose and Sam's _____ party, she only wanted to talk to Sam.

4. What is the _____ of the meeting this afternoon? I don't know if I can _____ make a decision if I do not have some advance notice of the topic.

Expand Your Learning

You learned in Chapter One that it is important to use a variety of strategies when learning and reviewing material. Do one or more of the following exercises to practice the words in this chapter.

Using your vision and color:

1. Write the words on note cards. Put the word on the front and the definition on the back. Use a different-color ink for the different categories of words according to the various word parts. To review the words, you should use three steps.
   a. Pronounce the word on the front.
   b. Try to remember the definition in your own words.
   c. Look at the back to check your answer.

   Separate the words into two piles, the ones you know and the ones you missed. Keep reviewing the ones you missed until you can recite them all correctly. You should repeat this several times during the week. Be sure to mix up the cards so you do not always do them in the same order.

2. Group the words according to their different word parts. Write each group in a different-color ink. Outline the shape of each word.

3. Draw simple stick figures to illustrate the meaning of each word.

4. Go back to the Fill in the Blank exercises and underline the context clues in each sentence that helped you identify the correct word.

5. Find other words that use the word parts in this chapter. Keep a list of words with each word part and add to it as you find more words throughout the semester.

Using your voice and hearing:

1. Make note cards as explained in the preceding exercise using vision. You do not need to use different-color inks unless you want to. When you go through the cards, say the words and the definitions out loud.

2. Go back to the Fill in the Blank exercises and read the sentences out loud. This would be a good way for you to check that you have used each word correctly.

Using large and small muscles:

1. Fold a piece of paper in half lengthwise and label the columns A and B. Write the words in column A and the definitions in B. Fold back column A and recite the words from the definitions; then do the reverse. Review the words as you do some sort of physical activity such as walking or riding an exercise bike.

2. Put the words and definitions on note cards as explained in the preceding exercise using vision. You do not need to use different-color inks unless you want to. Carry these cards with you and review them throughout the day as you do your daily activities such as brushing your teeth, eating breakfast, etc.

Puzzle Fun

Use what you know about this chapter's words to complete the puzzle. Read each hint carefully before answering.

Across

2. a synonym for this word is *recourse*
5. *release* is the opposite of this word
6. if it is not ordinary, it is _____
7. a synonym for this word is *transmit* or *radiate*
8. a synonym for this word is *surpass*
9. clear
13. very unassertive
14. an antonym for this word is *inhale*
15. if something is fair or unprejudiced, it is said to be this

Down

1. the definition for this word is exceeding a normal or proper limit
3. something that is dull is also said to be this
4. unable to see through
8. to empower is to do this
10. an antonym for this word is *fact* or *sense*
11. understanding or compassion
12. permits some light to pass through

CHAPTER EIGHT
Homonyms and Homophones

Words, like eyeglasses, blur everything they do not make clear.

Joseph Joubert, French moralist and essayist (1754–1824)

CHAPTER OBJECTIVE

Students will be able to identify and use words with the following common structural elements:

Roots: chrono
Prefixes: micro-, macro-, co-, con-, col-, com-

CHAPTER OUTLINE

 Memory Tip   Study Before Bed

 Vocabulary Strategy   Homonyms and Homophones

Part A
Words to Learn

chronological	microscope
chronic	microorganism
macroeconomics	macrocosm
microeconomics	

Structural Elements

chrono

macro-

micro-

Part B
Words to Learn

colleagues	coherent
cooperation	collaborate
convince	compromise
constituent	

Structural Elements

co-	col-
con-	com-

Power Words

spawn	analyze
synthesize	

Memory Tip   Study Before Bed

You will recall information better if you have less interference after your studying. Therefore, if you study before bed, go directly to sleep, and rehearse the information in the morning, your recall of information should be greater. This idea is interesting, although it is not a proven theory. Try it—see whether it works for you.

Vocabulary Strategy   Homonyms and Homophones

Homonyms are two or more words that have the same sound and often the same spelling but differ in meaning, such as to *bore* (as in "to cause someone to lose interest") and to *bore* ("to drill a hole").

Homophones are two or more words, such as *blue* and *blew*, that are pronounced the same but differ in meaning and spelling. Some people use the terms *homophone* and *homonym* interchangeably.

Here are examples of homophones:

1. *wave* and *waive*, *waver* and *waiver*
   a. *wave* (noun), a moving swell on the surface of a body of water
      The surfer rode the gigantic wave to shore.
      wave (verb), to sweep the hand or arm or some object
      The mother waved to her son as he got on the school bus.
   b. *waive* (verb), to relinquish
      The accused waived his rights to a preliminary hearing.
   c. *waver* (verb), to vacillate or move back and forth
      The vase wavered on the shelf before it fell to the floor and broke.
   d. *waiver* (noun), release or special exemption from a rule
      Most of the students tried to get waivers of their overdue fines.

2. *chorale* and *corral*
   a. *chorale* (noun), a type of hymn; a choir
      The patriotic chorale performed at the White House was very moving.
   b. *corral* (noun), a fenced enclosure for cattle or horses
      Two of the prized racehorses broke out of the corral because the fence was weak.
      corral (verb), to herd cattle or horses (or people) into one place
      Mia corralled Margaret into serving as secretary for the meetings.

Part A

WORDS TO LEARN—SEE AND SAY   Use the pronunciation guide on the first page of this book to help you SAY each word.

1. chronological   krŏn′ə-lŏj′ĭ-kəl
2. chronic   krŏn′ĭk
3. microscope   mī′krə-skōp′
4. microorganism   mī′krō-ôr′gə-nĭz′əm
5. microeconomics   mī′krō-ĕk′ə-nŏm′ĭks
6. macroeconomics   măk′rō-ĕk′ə-nŏm′ĭks
7. macrocosm   măk′rə-kŏz′əm

STRUCTURAL ELEMENTS

chrono	time
macro-	big, large
micro-	small

CONTEXT CLUES   Read the sentences. Use the words around the unfamiliar word to determine the word's meaning. Words in bold are the vocabulary words; words in italic are context clues.

1. On my vita I listed my jobs in **chronological** order, *from the earliest to my present job.*

2. Lenny has had **chronic** back pain *for the past 20 years.*

3. In science class Mitch used a **microscope** to *see the small organisms* in the water from the local river.

4. The **microorganism** was *so small it could not be seen with the naked eye.*

5. If you want to know the *detailed, inner workings* of a country's economy, ask your **microeconomics** professor.

6. In his **macroeconomics** class Bill studied the *overall trends* in economics over the past hundred years.

7. The **macrocosm** of his home and family was Dale's *universe*; it was all he knew at his young age.

 DICTIONARY   Read the following definitions.

1. **chronological**   krŏn′ə-lŏj′ĭ-kəl   adjective

   Etymology: chron (time) log (words) -al (relates to)

   Arranged in order of time occurrence

   The test scores were arranged in **chronological** order, starting with the *test taken at the beginning* of the semester.

2. **chronic**   krŏn′ĭk   adjective

   Etymology: chronic (time) ic (relates to)

   Relating to lasting a long period of time

   My doctor ordered several breathing tests before my **chronic** cough, which I have *had my entire life,* was diagnosed as asthma.

   Synonym: constant

   Antonym: intermittent

3. **microscope**   mī′krə-skōp′   noun

   Etymology: micro (small) scope (to see, an instrument)

   An instrument that enlarges small items or organisms so they are able to be seen

   The first **microscope** was used in 1650 and led to the discovery of the cell, which could not be seen with the human eye without *magnification.*

4. **microorganism**   mī′krō-ôr′gə-nĭz′əm   noun

   Etymology: micro (small) organism

   A very small living thing that you can see only with a microscope

   It is very important to wash your countertops after preparing chicken or other meats because of the **microorganisms** *that you cannot see* but that might contaminate other food.

5. **microeconomics**   mī′krō-ĕk′ə-nŏm′ĭks   noun

   Etymology: micro (small) economics

   The study of the individual operations of the components of the national economy, such as individuals, households, or consumers

   When studying **microeconomics** you will analyze basic market trends for *small areas* of the country.

6. **macroeconomics**   măk′rō-ĕk′ə-nŏm′ĭks   noun

   Etymology: macro (big) economics

The study of the overall aspects and workings of a national economy as a whole; for example, total income, total employment, and unemployment

The *gross national product and national unemployment rate are examples* of topics that one would study when taking **macroeconomics**.

7. **macrocosm**   măk′rə-kŏz′əm   noun

Etymology: macro (big) cosm (world)

The entire world; the universe; a system reflecting on a large scale one of its component systems or parts

The study of our **macrocosm** led to many new discoveries that would never have known without this study examining the *entire universe*.

Synonym: universe

Practice Exercises

MULTIPLE CHOICE

1. Which of the following is in <u>chronological</u> order?
    a. 5, 10, 8, 7, 3, 15
    b. English, Science, Psychology, Research Writing
    c. getting your car repaired, eating dinner, cooking breakfast
    d. Monday, Tuesday, Wednesday, Thursday, Friday

2. Which of the following statements would describe a <u>chronic</u> problem?
    a. This has been going on for as long as I can remember.
    b. This just started yesterday.
    c. Last week my knee hurt, now it is my toe.
    d. Everything was fine until I changed the flat tire.

3. Which of the following would you study in a <u>macroeconomics</u> class?
    a. individual details that increase profits to a business
    b. unilateral versus bilateral decisions in business
    c. the big picture
    d. the effect of revolution on a country's economy

4. Which of the following would you study in a <u>microeconomics</u> class?
    a. individual details that increase profits to a business
    b. unilateral versus bilateral decisions in business
    c. the big picture
    d. the effect of revolution on a country's economy

5. Why would you use a <u>microscope</u>?
    a. to study the solar system
    b. to examine living organisms in river water
    c. to examine the eating habits of field mice
    d. to see wild animals from a far distance

6. How could you see a <u>microorganism</u>?
    a. with binoculars
    b. with 3D glasses
    c. with a telescope
    d. with a microscope

7. If you examined our <u>macrocosm</u>, what would you look at?
   a. individual cells
   b. earth and how it fits into the solar system
   c. our national parks and how to preserve them
   d. the effects of increased gasoline consumption on the economy

FILL IN THE BLANK Select the **BEST** word for each sentence. Use each word only once.

chronological   chronic   microscope   microeconomics
microorganisms   macroeconomics macrocosm

1. The doctors diagnosed Tom's problem as _____ because it had been going on for many years.

2. I wanted to see whether there was a difference between blonde and brown hair, so I examined the hairs using a _____.

3. Jenna was so fearful of germs that she cleaned everything she touched in order to kill all of the _____.

4. Because of her interest in the solar system, Jenny took a class that said it would study our _____.

5. When trying to find her missing wallet, Jane thought about what she had done that day in _____ order from morning to evening.

6. Bill wanted to run his own company, so he studied _____ in order to understand how one small change in the business structure would impact his profits.

7. Bill wanted to run his own company, so he studied _____ in order to understand how competition works in a capitalist society

CORRECT OR INCORRECT? If the sentence is correct, write a "C" on the line provided. If not, write an "I" for incorrect, then REWRITE the sentence to make it correct. You can change any part of the sentence to make it correct.

1. To make grocery shopping easier, I write out my list in <u>chronological</u> order according to the store's floor plan.

   _____

2. Matt took his dog to the veterinarian because of a <u>chronic</u> cough that started yesterday.

   _____

3. Using her knowledge of <u>macroeconomics</u>, Sue was able to analyze the inconsistent pay increases throughout the company's records.

   _____

4. After her <u>microeconomics</u> class, Karen understood how a change in the price of one item affected the sales number for a similar item across the board.

   _____

5. Joanie used the <u>microscope</u> in her science kit to examine how her dolls were constructed.

   _____

6. The <u>microorganisms</u> in the river water were so big the scientists could pick them up in their fingers.

   _____

7. When studying the <u>macrocosm</u> of anyone's world, you would examine the day-to-day individual aspects of that person's life.

   _____

SHORT ANSWER   Write your answers on a separate sheet of paper.

1. List what you do in a typical day in <u>chronological</u> order.

2. <u>Chronic</u> generally has a negative tone. But what are three positive things about you that are <u>chronic</u>? For example, are you a <u>chronic</u> book buyer?

3. Think about your personal expenses. Which would be considered in a study of <u>microeconomics</u> and in a study of <u>macroeconomics</u>? Why?

4. Name three things you could examine using a <u>microscope</u>.

5. Name three places where you might come in contact with <u>microorganisms</u> throughout your day.

6. Consider you own <u>macrocosm</u>. What are your favorite aspects?

Part B

 WORDS TO LEARN—SEE AND SAY   Use the pronunciation guide on the first page of this book to help you SAY each word.

1. colleagues   kŏl′ĕgz′

2. cooperation   kō-ŏp′ə-rā′shən

3. convince   kən-vĭns′

4. constituent   kən-stĭch′ōō-ənt

5. collaborate   kə-lăb′ə-rāt′

6. coherent   kō-hîr′ənt

7. compromise   kŏm′prə-mīz′

 STRUCTURAL ELEMENTS   Look at the structural elements of each word. Use these elements to unlock the word's meaning.

  col-, con-, co-, com-   together, together with

 CONTEXT CLUES   Read the sentences. Use the words around the unfamiliar word to determine the meaning. Words in bold are the vocabulary words; words in italic are context clues.

1. My **colleagues**, *Andrea, Jeremy, and Denise*, helped me prepare the final report for the board meeting last week.

2. It is important to have the **cooperation** and *support* of your superior when trying to make significant changes.

3. Eric was trying to **convince** his mother that the movie *was appropriate* for a ten-year-old to view *so she would let him go with his friends*.

4. Lauren was saying that the *two* **constituents** essential for happiness are *the ability to laugh and the ability to see one's self through the eyes of others*.

5. The teacher told the *two classes* to **collaborate** on the project and *work together*.

6. After Dennis's accident he was unable to have a **coherent** conversation with anyone; *it took him about six months before he could express himself clearly*.

7. Sally wanted to stay out until 11:00 PM and her parents wanted her home at 9:00 PM, so they **compromised** and *settled on the middle ground* of 10:00 PM.

DICTIONARY   Read the following definitions.

1. **colleagues**   kŏl′ĕgz′   noun

    Etymology: col (with) legare (to choose)

    Fellow members of a profession or staff; associates

Dr. Jones consulted with his **colleagues** *who worked with him* before recommending surgery for the young girl.

Synonyms: peer, coworker

2. **cooperation**   kō-ŏp′ə-rā′shən   noun

Etymology: co (with, together with) operate (work)

The act of working together on a common enterprise or project

Parents and teachers must *work together* and show **cooperation** when dealing with matters of discipline and academics.

Synonyms: alliance, collaboration

3. **convince**   kən-vĭns′   verb

Etymology: con (with, together with) vinc (to conquer)

Make someone agree, understand, or realize the truth or validity of something

The doctor had to **convince** the patient that surgery was the only choice for him and *help him understand* that it was necessary.

Synonyms: persuade, argue

4. **constituent**   kən-stĭch′ōō-ənt   noun

Etymology: con (together with) stit or stat (stand) -ent (something that or someone who)

A component; a resident of a district or member of a group represented by an elected official

Since his reelection, Senator Brown offered the **constituents** *in his district* his appreciation and sincerely promised to continue to support their causes.

Synonyms: factor, prime unit

5. **collaborate**   kə-lăb′ə-rāt′   verb

Etymology: col (with, together with) labor (work) ate (to make or cause to be)

To work together

Dr. Smith asked me to **collaborate** *with him* on the research project.

6. **coherent**   kō-hîr′ənt   adjective

Etymology: co (with, together with) her (stick)

Sticking together; marked by an orderly, logical relationship of parts

Because she made such a **coherent** *and logical* argument, her plan was accepted by the board.

Synonyms: understandable, logical

7. **compromise**   kŏm′prə-mīz′   verb

Etymology: com (together) promise

To solve a problem or end an argument in which both people or groups accept that they cannot have everything they want

I wanted Chinese food, but my boyfriend wanted Italian, so we *each gave in* and **compromised** on an American restaurant.

Synonyms: agree, negotiate

Antonyms: disagree, resist

Practice Exercises

MULTIPLE CHOICE

1. Where would you most likely see your <u>colleagues</u>?
    a. at the bowling alley
    b. while mowing your grass
    c. on vacation
    d. in your workplace

2. Which of the following phrases would indicate <u>cooperation</u>?
    a. "Let me help you with that."
    b. "I can do it myself, thank you."
    c. "Give me your part of the project as soon as possible."
    d. "Call me when you are done."

3. Which classroom activity is an example of <u>collaborative</u> learning?
    a. taking a test by yourself
    b. discussing the answers to a problem in a group
    c. journal writing
    d. predicting test questions

4. How could someone <u>convince</u> you to change your mind?
    a. make up an unbelievable story
    b. try to blackmail you
    c. tell you facts to prove his or her point
    d. ignore all your requests to talk

5. What would be a characteristic of a <u>coherent</u> story?
    a. It would be easily understood.
    b. It would have a lot of extra detail.
    c. It would have a lot of big words that you do not know.
    d. It would have a happy ending.

6. Which of the following means the same as <u>constituent</u>?
    a. the whole
    b. the parts
    c. the leftovers
    d. to mix together

7. What would someone say if he or she were willing to <u>compromise</u>?
    a. "I will not budge on inch."
    b. "It's my way or the highway."
    c. "I'll give a little if you'll give a little."
    d. "You'll have to give in. I will not."

FILL IN THE BLANK   Select the BEST answer for each sentence. Use each word only once.

colleagues	compromised	cooperation	collaborate
convince	coherent	constituents	

1. Jerry wanted to stay out until midnight, but his parents wanted him home by 10:00 PM. They _____ and settled on 11:00 PM.

2. I worked with my _____ on the project, so we all shared in the acknowledgment.

3. Betty did not want to go on a date with Jack, so he sent flowers and candy to try to _____ her to change her mind.

4. The ringing telephone woke Jackie up from her nap; therefore, she was not _____ when she answered the call.

5. A marriage works best if there is a spirit of _____; if husband and wife work together, the household will run smoothly.

6. In your classes you may have to _____ with other students when you are assigned a group project.

7. The county's representative on the city council met with her _____ to see how they wanted her to vote on the tax increase.

CORRECT OR INCORRECT?   If the sentence is correct, write a "C" on the line provided. If not, write an "I" for incorrect, then REWRITE the sentence to make it correct. You can change any part of the sentence to make it correct.

1. The governing party refused to <u>compromise</u>. It agreed to several of the demands made by the revolutionary party.

   _____

2. After years of working together, my <u>colleagues</u> and I decided to start our own business.

   _____

3. In the spirit of <u>cooperation</u>, the rival gangs continued to fight with each other and harass the people in the neighborhoods.

   _____

4. I hope this last speeding ticket will <u>convince</u> you to obey the speed limit.

   _____

5. Jim had a hard time taking lecture notes, so he preferred a professor who was not <u>coherent</u> in his lecture style.

   _____

6. The traitor <u>collaborated</u> with the enemy and was assassinated when his countrymen discovered his crime.

   _____

7. There are many <u>constituents</u> that make up a complete course of study for a liberal arts degree.

   _____

SHORT ANSWER   Write your answers on a separate sheet of paper.

1. What information about a friend would <u>convince</u> you to lend him or her your car?
2. Who are your <u>colleagues</u>?
3. Name three times when you or someone you know had to <u>compromise</u>.
4. How would someone act if he or she were <u>cooperating</u> on a group project?
5. Name two things that are easier to do if you can <u>collaborate</u> with other students.
6. Write a sentence that is *not* <u>coherent</u>.
7. Explain the role that the <u>constituents</u> might play in an upcoming election.

Power Words

1. **spawn**   spôn   verb

   To produce in large numbers

   The recent passing of the gambling bill is said to have **spawned** *crime and financial havoc throughout the state.*

   Synonyms: generate, originate, reproduce

2. **analyze**   ăn′ə-līz′   verb

   To examine by separating into parts

   It is important to **analyze** *your reasons for taking* the sales position *as opposed to* taking the office manager's job.

   Synonyms: evaluate, interpret

3. **synthesize**   sĭn′thĭ-sīz′   verb

   To combine; to form a new, complex product; to put together

   After reading both research reports, **synthesize** your findings *into a one-page summary.*

   Synonyms: blend, incorporate, integrate

Practice Exercises

1. Describe a situation in which you would be asked to <u>analyze</u> data.

2. Describe a situation in which you would be asked to <u>synthesize</u> information. (Try to think of a situation that does not involve your college work.)

3. Relate the word <u>spawn</u> to something other than eggs or children. What else could you <u>spawn</u>?

Chapter Review

Yes or No?

Read the sentence and answer the question.

1. Sam's <u>colleagues</u> had no spirit of <u>cooperation</u>.

   a. Is Sam referring to his friends? _____

   b. Did they work well together? _____

2. His advisors <u>convinced</u> the senator to vote the way his <u>constituents</u> wanted.

   a. Did the senator follow his advisors' advice? _____

   b. Did the senator listen to his voters? _____

3. The <u>coherent</u> essay answer <u>convinced</u> the professor that the student understood the topic.

   a. Was the answer easy to understand? _____

   b. Was the professor satisfied with the student's knowledge of the topic? _____

4. The town's spirit of <u>cooperation</u> helped overcome the devastation left by the flood.

   a. Did the people in the town work together? _____

5. Lisa tried to <u>convince</u> Jamison to see a new doctor about his <u>chronic</u> back pain.

   a. Did Lisa want Jamison to do something? _____

   b. Was Jamison's back pain new? _____

6. The two political parties agreed to <u>compromise</u> and choose one scientist to examine the town's water supply for <u>microorganisms</u>.

   a. Did the two parties continue to argue? _____

   b. Was the scientist looking for fish in the water? _____

Expanded Word Forms

cooperate	cooperation	cooperating	chronological	chronologically
convince	convincing	convinced		

1. Helping toddlers get dressed is much easier if they _____. Their _____ is necessary to get their shoes on correctly. If they are _____, the job will be done much more quickly.

2. Joe was very _____ when he was apologizing to Sue. He was trying to _____ her that he had a good excuse for missing their date. She was not _____ and refused to see him again.

3. Mrs. Martin introduced her children _____, from the youngest to the oldest. She had them stand in _____ order so the guest could easily identify each one.

Expand Your Learning

You learned in Chapter One that it is important to use a variety of strategies when learning and reviewing material. Do one or more of the following exercises to practice the words in this chapter.

Using your vision and color:

1. Write the words on note cards. Put the word on the front and the definition on the back. Use a different-color ink for the different categories of words according to the various word parts. To review the words, you should use three steps.
   a. Pronounce the word on the front.
   b. Try to remember the definition in your own words.
   c. Look at the back to check your answer.

   Separate the words into two piles, the ones you know and the ones you missed. Keep reviewing the ones you missed until you can recite them all correctly. You should repeat this several times during the week. Be sure to mix up the cards so you do not always do them in the same order.

2. Group the words according to their different word parts. Write each group in a different-color ink. Outline the shape of each word.

3. Draw simple stick figures to illustrate the meaning of each word.

4. Go back to the Fill in the Blank exercises and underline the context clues in each sentence that helped you identify the correct word.

5. Find other words that use the word parts in this chapter. Keep a list of words with each word part and add to it as you find more words throughout the semester.

Using your voice and hearing:

1. Make note cards as explained in the preceding exercise using vision. You do not need to use different-color inks unless you want to. When you go through the cards, say the words and the definitions out loud.

2. Go back to the Fill in the Blank exercises and read the sentences out loud. This would be a good way for you to check that you have used each word correctly.

Using large and small muscles:

1. Fold a piece of paper in half lengthwise and label the columns A and B. Write the words in column A and the definitions in B. Fold back column A and recite the words from the definitions, then do the reverse. Review the words as you do some sort of physical activity such as walking or riding an exercise bike.

2. Put the words and definitions on note cards as explained in the preceding exercise using vision. You do not need to use different-color inks unless you want to. Carry these cards with you and review them throughout the day as you do your daily activities such as brushing your teeth, eating breakfast, etc.

Puzzle Fun

Read the sentence. Select the BEST vocabulary word for each sentence and write the word in the puzzle.

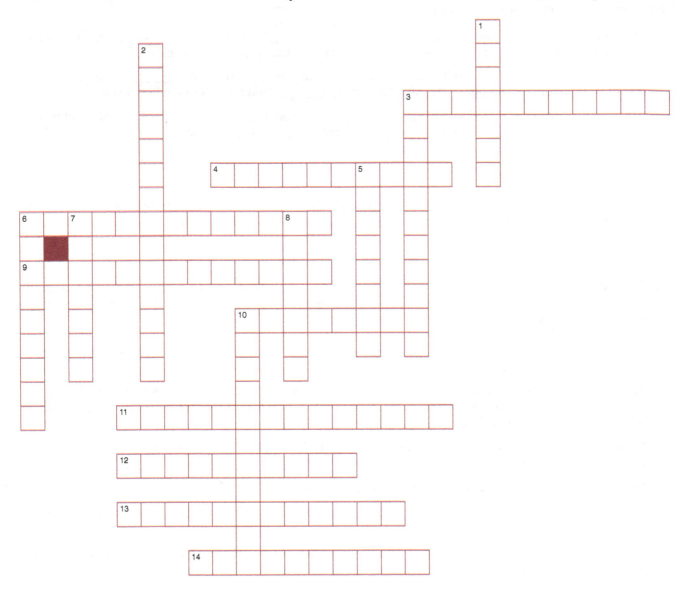

Across

3. Dr. Smith asked me to _____ with him on the research project.
4. In science class Mitch used a _____ to see the small organisms in the water from the local river.
6. The _____ was so small it could not be seen with the naked eye.
9. On my vita I listed my jobs in _____ order, from the earliest to my present job.
10. The doctor had to _____ the patient that surgery was the only choice for him and help him understand that it was necessary.
11. In his _____ class Bill studied the overall trends in economics over the past hundred years.

Down

1. It is important to _____ your reasons for taking the sales position as opposed to taking the office manager's job.
2. If you want to know the detailed, inner workings of a country's economy, ask your _____ professor.
3. Sally wanted to stay out until 11:00 PM and her parents wanted her home at 9:00 PM, so they _____ and settled on the middle ground of 10:00 PM.
5. Because she made such a _____ and logical argument, her plan was accepted by the board.
6. The _____ of his home and family was Dale's universe; it was all he knew at his young age.

12. My _____, Andrea, Jeremy, and Denise, helped me prepare the final report for the board meeting last week.

13. Since his reelection, Mayor Brown offered his _____ his appreciation and sincerely promised to continue to support their causes.

14. After reading both research reports, _____ your findings into a one-page summary.

7. Lenny has had _____ back pain for the past 20 years.

8. The recent passing of the gambling bill is said to have _____ crime and financial havoc throughout the state.

10. Parents and teachers must work together and show _____ when dealing with matters of discipline and academics.

CHAPTER NINE
Don't Let Words Confuse You

The word is half his that speaks, and half his that hears it.

Michael de Montaigne, French author (1533–1592)

CHAPTER OBJECTIVE

Student will be able to identify and use words with the following common structural elements:

Roots: therm
Prefixes: auto-, tele-, phono-, mal-, bene-
Suffixes: -ible

CHAPTER OUTLINE

 Memory Tip   Use Multiple Senses to Enhance Learning

 Vocabulary Strategy   Confusing Words

Part A
Words to Learn

autobiography	flexible
autograph	compatible
autonomy	
thermal	
thermostat	

Structural Elements

auto-

therm

-ible

Part B
Words to Learn

phonics	telecommunication
phoneme	telepathy
benefactor	malefactor
beneficiary	malice

Structural Elements

tele-

phono-

mal-

bene-

Power Words

hone	nuance
bevy	

💡 *Memory Tip*   Use Multiple Senses to Enhance Learning

If you can involve as many senses as possible when studying and learning, you will learn faster and more effectively. Our senses are seeing, hearing, touching, smelling, tasting. The chapter section Expand Your Learning describes some strategies you can use involving your senses. Here are some other ideas to incorporate your senses into your learning:

- *Seeing*—Visualize pictures to connect to the words; look for magazine or clip art pictures to illustrate each word.

- *Hearing*—Say the words out loud, read the sentence out loud, and read the exercises out loud as you are completing them.

- *Touch*—Write the words and their definitions; use study cards.

- *Smell*—This is tough one, but maybe you can have a particular candle you light when you are studying and that scent will trigger the mental idea of studying.

- *Taste*—Suck on a flavor of candy while studying such as peppermint, then eat that same type of candy while taking the test.

🔍 *Vocabulary Strategy*   Confusing Words

Many times students know what they want to say, but are confused by which word is correct. Below are several pairs of confusing words that students often misuse. See whether you know the correct word to put in the blank. The answers are provided at the end of this chapter.

Threw is the past tense of throw; *through* means to go in one side and out the other.

- Yesterday Billy _____ his baseball _____ his neighbor's window.

There indicates a location; *their* indicates ownership.

- Put your books over _____ by the window.
- The Smiths always kept _____ dog on a leash.

Due is a deadline, when something should be done; *do* refers to taking action.

- The final paper is _____ May 1.
- What would you like to _____ this evening?

Then refers to a point in time, usually after something else; *than* refers to a comparison.

- First Joe went to the gym, _____ he will stop at the bank.
- I would rather play tennis _____ baseball.

Additional Confusing Words

- *affect* and *effect*
  - **affect:** change, influence
  - **effect:** to bring about (verb); result, impression (noun)

- *capital* and *capitol*
  - **capital:** seat of government; money; uppercase letters
  - **capitol:** building where legislative body meets

- *accept* and *except*
  - **accept:** receive
  - **except:** exclude

- *lay* and *lie*
  - **lay:** to set down, to place or put down an item
  - **lie:** to recline

- *principal* and *principle*
    - **principal:** first in authority; main participant; amount of a debt less interest
    - **principle:** basic truth or assumption

Try writing a sentence using each of the confusing words above. You will find that it isn't as easy as it appears to be.

Part A

 WORDS TO LEARN—SEE AND SAY   Use the pronunciation guide on the first page of this book to help you SAY each word.

1. autobiography   ô′tō-bī-ŏg′rə-fē
2. autograph   ô′tə-grăf′
3. autonomy   ô-tŏn′ə-mē
4. thermal   thûr′məl
5. thermostat   thûr′mə-stăt′
6. flexible   flĕk′sə-bəl
7. compatible   kəm-păt′ə-bəl

 STRUCTURAL ELEMENTS   Look at the structural elements of each word. Use these elements to unlock the word's meaning.

auto-	self
therm	heat
-ible	able, capable of, fit for

CONTEXT CLUES   Read the sentences. Use the words around the unfamiliar word to determine the word's meaning. Words in bold are the vocabulary words; words in italic are context clues.

1. George wrote his **autobiography,** *the story of his own life,* because he did not trust anyone else to write the complete truth.

2. Mike was happy to receive an **autographed** baseball jersey for his birthday. Jerseys with the *player's signature* are always worth more than a plain jersey.

3. The private college administrators wanted complete **autonomy.** They wanted to *make their own decisions* without having to answer to another governing group.

4. Doris loved the **thermal** blanket she received as a graduation gift. Even though her room was cold, the blanket *kept her warm.*

5. Diane's new apartment is hot, but she cannot *control the temperature* because the **thermostat** is in the owner's apartment, not hers.

6. Joan's children all love the **flexible,** *bendable,* straws.

7. Jeff was annoyed because his new mobile phone was not **compatible** with his old phone's cord. They did not *fit together.*

 DICTIONARY   Read the following definitions.

1. **autobiography**   ô′tō-bī-ŏg′rə-fē   noun

    Etymology: auto (self) bio (life or living things) graphy (something written)

    The story of a person's life written by that person; written account of one's life

I am waiting for the release of the president's **autobiography** because I want to read the *account of his presidencey in his own words.*

Synonyms: journal, memoirs

2. **autograph**   ô′tə-grăf′   noun

Etymology: auto (self) graph (something written)

A person's own signature or handwriting

The *signature* on the celebrity's check did not match the **autograph** he had given at the concert.

Synonym: signature

Vocabulary Tip: An original manuscript or musical composition written in the handwriting of the author or composer is also called an **autograph**.

3. **autonomy**   ô-tŏn′ə-mē   noun

Etymology: auto (self) nomos (regulating or laws)

The condition or quality of being independent of rule of governments or others; self-governing

The **autonomy**, *or independence*, that teenagers desire often turns out to be not as desirable compared to when they were dependent upon their parents and had them for support and guidance.

Synonyms: freedom, liberty

Antonym: dependence

4. **thermal**   thûr′məl   adjective

Etymology: therm (heat) al (relates to)

Of, relating to, using, producing, or caused by heat

Wearing a **thermal** shirt under your sweater *helps keep you warm* on a brutally cold day.

5. **thermostat**   thûr′mə-stăt′   noun

Etymology: therm (heat) stat (stand)

A piece of equipment that controls the temperature in a building, machine, or engine

Because the bedroom is on the second floor of our condo, it's usually warmer than the *temperature set* on the **thermostat** downstairs.

Synonym: regulator

6. **flexible**   flĕk′sə-bəl   adjective

Etymology: flex (to bend) ible (capable of)

Capable of being bent or flexed; responsive to change

The **flexible** drinking straw was invented in 1930 by a man who saw his daughter *struggling to drink with a straight* paper straw. (vocabulary.com)

Synonyms: pliable, adaptable

7. **compatible**   kəm-păt′ə-bəl   adjective

Etymology: com (together, together with) pati (to suffer, to do) ible (able)

Able to live or function in harmony and without conflict

Denise and Dennis knew their personalities were very **compatible** and that was why they were such *great friends.*

Synonyms: harmonious, agreeable, congruent

Antonyms: unsuited, imcompatible

Practice Exercises

MULTIPLE CHOICE

1. Who would write your <u>autobiography</u>?
   a. your best friend
   b. your worst enemy
   c. yourself
   d. your parents

2. If an author <u>autographs</u> his new novel, what does he do?
   a. reads part of the book out loud to people in the audience
   b. signs his name inside the book
   c. deposits his royalty check
   d. sells the book to people who come to see him

3. If you have <u>autonomy</u>, who would decide when you should come home from a date?
   a. your parents
   b. yourself
   c. your date
   d. your best friend

4. John bought <u>thermal</u> clothing in order to
   a. stay cool in hot temperatures
   b. stay warm in cold temperatures
   c. stay dry in wet weather
   d. all of the above

5. When would you adjust your <u>thermostat</u>?
   a. when you wanted it to get cold outside so it would snow
   b. when your house or apartment was too hot
   c. when the kitchen floor needed to be scrubbed
   d. when you wanted to be alone

6. Which of the following can be <u>flexible</u>?
   a. a soft rubber pipe
   b. a steel beam
   c. your ideas about your career
   d. both a and c
   e. all of the above

7. How would you describe a <u>compatible</u> person?
   a. pushy, single-minded
   b. set in his or her ways
   c. always wants to be in charge and say how things are done
   d. pleasant, easy to work with

FILL IN THE BLANK   Select the BEST answer for each sentence. Use each word only once.

| autobiography | autonomy | autograph | thermostat |
| flexible | compatible | thermal | |

1. The police were able to find the missing girl in the woods by using _____, or body heat, imaging.

2. Jerry went to the _____ session at the stadium because he wanted to get his jersey signed by his favorite player.

3. The first part of Samuel Clemens's _____, the story of his life in his own words, was released in 2010.

4. John found that he and Joan were very _____. They worked together well and agreed on the decisions that had to be made.

5. Sarah adjusted the _____ in her house when the temperature dropped and it was cold.

6. When she turned 18, Cheryl had _____ and was able to make her own decisions.

7. Sybil's parents were _____ and allowed her to come home sometime between 11:00 PM and midnight.

CORRECT OR INCORRECT?   If the sentence is correct, write a "C" on the line provided. If not, write an "I" for incorrect, then REWRITE the sentence to make it correct. You can change any part of the sentence to make it correct.

1. Walter Isaacson wrote Steve Jobs's <u>autobiography</u>, which was published shortly after Jobs's death in 2011.

   _____

2. When they were rescued after being lost in the desert in 100 degree heat, Joe and Jane were wrapped in <u>thermal</u> blankets to lower their body heat.

   _____

3. The <u>thermostat</u> is connected to your furnace and air-conditioning unit. It can be adjusted to make your house warmer or cooler.

   _____

4. Each sorority on campus had <u>autonomy</u>, and all had to abide by the decisions made by the nationwide council of presidents.

   _____

5. The company's regulations on work hours were <u>flexible</u>—employees could decide to come into the office or work at home.

   _____

6. Carol was infuriated at Don because he was so <u>compatible</u>.

   _____

7. On eBay, Joe bought a baseball <u>autographed</u> by Mickey Mantle.

   _____

SHORT ANSWER   Write your answers on a separate sheet of paper.

1. What are three key events in your life so far that you would include in your <u>autobiography</u>?

2. In what areas of your life do you have <u>autonomy</u>? What decisions do you make?

3. When would you like to have a <u>thermal</u> blanket? When would you not want one?

4. What do you think is the ideal setting for your home or apartment <u>thermostat</u> in the summer? In the winter?

5. What are three rules at your school that you wish were <u>flexible</u>? Why?

6. Name three people you are <u>compatible</u> with and would like to work with on a class project. What qualities do they possess that make them compatible?

7. Think of some of your possessions. Which three would you like to have someone <u>autograph</u>? Why?

Part B

  WORDS TO LEARN—SEE AND SAY   Use the pronunciation guide on the first page of this book to help you SAY each word.

1. phonics   fŏn′ĭks
2. phoneme   fō′nēm′
3. telepathy   tə-lĕp′ə-thē
4. telecommunications   te-li-kə-′myü-nə-′kā-shən
5. benefactor   bĕn′ə-făk′tər
6. beneficiary   bĕn′ə-fĭsh′ē-ĕr′ē
7. malefactor   măl′ə-făk′tər
8. malice   măl′ĭs

  STRUCTURAL ELEMENTS   Look at the structural elements of each word. Use these elements to unlock the word's meaning.

tele-	from a distance
phono-	sound
mal-	bad
bene-	good

CONTEXT CLUES   Read the sentences. Use the words around the unfamiliar word to determine the word's meaning. Words in bold are the vocabulary words; words in italic are context clues.

1. Megan's first-grade teacher taught her **phonics,** so she is very good at *sounding out new words* she does not know.

2. When Ellie was learning to read, she liked to make rhyming words by changing the beginning **phoneme**, or *letter that has its own sound*, to make a new word.

3. In the movie, the aliens were able to communicate by **telepathy** *without speaking*.

4. *Telephones, cell phones, and television* are all forms of **telecommunication**.

5. The anonymous **benefactor** *provided enough money* for the library to expand its hours.

6. The *library* was the **beneficiary** *of the anonymous gift of money*.

7. After the **malefactor** was *arrested,* the community groups praised the police for their fast work in solving the crime.

8. After his conviction, the malefactor said he was sorry he had *acted in* **malice** and for the *harm he caused* his neighbors.

  DICTIONARY   Read the following definitions.

1. **phonics**   fŏn′ĭks   noun

   Etymology: phon (sound) ic (relates or pertains to)

   A method of teaching reading and spelling based on the interpretation of the spelling, letter placement, and letter sounds

   Many early elementary teachers promote the teaching of **phonics**, which helps students *break down words into their simplest unit,* as opposed to whole language, which works with whole words.

2. **phoneme**   fō′nēm′   noun

   Etymology: phon (sound) eme (unit of)

   The smallest phonetic unit in a language that is capable of conveying a distinction in meaning; for example, the *m* in *mat* and the *b* in *bat* in English

   Many **phonemes** are difficult for the hearing impaired students because since they can't clearly hear the *sound made by the letter.*

3. **telepathy**   tə-lĕp′ə-thē   noun

   Etymology: tele (from a distance) pathy (feelings)

   Communication from one mind to another by extrasensory means; communicating through means other than the five senses (see the Memory Tip in this chapter for these senses)

   Many people believe that identical twins have a special **telepathy** whereby they can *feel each other's pain or know what their sibling is thinking.*

   Synonyms: clairvoyance, premonition

4. **telecommunication**   te-li-ke-′myü-ne-′kā-shen   noun

   Etymology: tele (from a distance) communicate

   The science and technology of communication at a distance by electronic transmission of impulses, as by telegraph, cable, telephone, radio, television, email, etc.

   The *Internet* is the most recent *technology* that uses **telecommunication** to *transmit messages.*

5. **benefactor**   bĕn′ə-făk′tər   noun

   Etymology: bene (good) fac (to make) or (something or someone who)

   One that gives aid, especially financial aid

   I could not have gone to college without the support of my *aunt*, who was a generous **benefactor** and *paid for my tuition.*

   Synonym: sponsor

   Antonyms: opponent, beneficiary

6. **beneficiary**   bĕn′ə-fĭsh′ē-ĕr′ē   noun

   Etymology: bene (good) fic (make) -iary (receiver of)

   The recipient of funds, property, or other benefits; often from an insurance policy or will

   After winning the lottery I named my *niece* as my **beneficiary** to *inherit the money* in the event of my untimely death.

   Synonyms: receiver, grantee

   Antonym: giver

7. **malefactor**   măl′ə-făk′tər   noun

   Etymology: mal (bad) fac (to make) of (something or someone who)

   One that has committed a crime

   Prisons are full of **malefactors** who *have committed terrible crimes* against society.

   Synonyms: evildoer, criminal, villian

   Antonyms: benefactor, do-gooder

8. **malice**   măl′ĭs   noun

   Etymology: mal (bad) ice (something caused to be)

   A desire to harm others or to see others suffer

Jeremy said, "I'm so sorry my *comments got you fired*; I really didn't intend any **malice**. I was just joking with you."

Synonym: spite

Antonym: kindness

Practice Exercises

MULTIPLE CHOICE

1. Which of the following is an example of a <u>phonics</u> rule?
   a. Context clues help you find the meaning of words.
   b. Always use spell check on your computer when writing papers.
   c. Study cards are a good strategy to help learn new words.
   d. Silent *e* at the end of a word makes the middle vowel long.

2. Which of the following are examples of <u>phonemes</u>?
   a. mat, cat, sat, hat
   b. m, c, s, h
   c. shall, then, when
   d. sh, th, wh
   e. both b and d
   f. all of the above

3. If you had the ability of <u>telepathy</u>, you could communicate
   a. clearly through a fast-food restaurant drive-up speaker
   b. quickly by text message
   c. silently without speaking
   d. loudly above all the noise on a school bus

4. Which of the following are means of <u>telecommunication</u>?
   a. mobile phones
   b. instant messaging
   c. email
   d. both b and c
   e. all of the above

5. What would a <u>benefactor</u> do?
   a. wash your car for you
   b. do your grocery shopping
   c. give you money to pay for your books
   d. both a and b
   e. all of the above

6. If you were someone's <u>beneficiary</u>, what might you receive?
   a. a bill for repairing your car
   b. money to pay for your car repair
   c. a request to help with his or her income taxes
   d. advice about what courses to take next semester

7. Where would you find many <u>malefactors</u>?
   a. at the grocery store
   b. in jail
   c. on the Internet
   d. sitting next to you in class

8. Which of the following would be a statement said in <u>malice</u>?
    a. "I like your new car."
    b. "Could you help me with my homework?"
    c. "I hate you!"
    d. "Would you like to go out for dinner Saturday night?"

FILL IN THE BLANK   Select the BEST word for each sentence. Use each word only once.

phonics	phoneme	malefactor	malice
telepathy	telecommunication	benefactor	beneficiary

1. My _____ was very generous and bought me a new car when my old one quit running.

2. My great-grandfather would be amazed at how _____ has developed so that now we can talk to our relatives in a different country while riding in our car.

3. The neighbors were glad to see the police arrest the _____ who was breaking into cars on their street.

4. Sending a message through _____ means you are communicating with your minds. No one is speaking.

5. Be careful not to say anything with _____ when you are angry. People often don't forget something hurtful that is said to them.

6. When Miles was learning to speak, he would mix up the _____ at the beginning of words and sometimes said, "baddy" for "Daddy."

7. Marie was grateful to her aunt who made her the _____ in her will. Because of the gift Marie was able to pay off her school loans.

8. In first grade, Susie's teacher taught her _____ rules to help her sound out new words.

CORRECT OR INCORRECT?   If the sentence is correct, write a "C" on the line provided. If not, write an "I" for incorrect, then REWRITE the sentence to make it correct. You may change any part of the sentence to make it correct.

1. In order to be an effective elementary teacher, Ellie had to learn about <u>phonics</u> and how to teach the subject to her students.

   _____

2. When James was practicing his spelling words, he tried to learn them by looking at the <u>phonemes,</u> the number and shapes of the letters in each word.

   _____

3. The <u>malefactor</u> did so much good in the community that a street was named after him.

   _____

4. Jolene was such a kind person; she always spoke with <u>malice</u> against others.

   _____

5. Dale wanted to be a magician, so he kept trying to communicate using <u>telepathy</u> to guess the audience's secrets.

   _____

6. Jerome thinks that <u>telecommunication</u> such as letter writing has changed the way information is shared.

   _____

7. The summer camp's <u>benefactor</u> gave money every summer for children who could not afford the fees.

   _____

8. Sammy was sent to jail because he was the <u>beneficiary</u> in his uncle's will.

   _____

SHORT ANSWER   Write your answers on a separate sheet of paper.

1. One <u>phonics</u> rule is that when two consonants are together in the middle of a word, that is where the word is divided into syllables. For example, there are two syllables in the word *hammer* (*ham* and *mer*) and two syllables in the word *silver* (*sil* and *ver*). List four other words that have double consonants in the middle and two syllables.

2. From the following words, see how many new words you can make by changing the beginning or ending <u>phoneme</u>.
   a. bat
   b. boat
   c. day

3. Put *tele-* in the center of a concept map and words that contain that word part around the center of the map. Add additional words that are not in this chapter.

4. *Bene-* and *mal-* have opposite meanings. Construct a concept map to show the meaning of the words in this chapter. Then add more words with the two prefixes along with their definitions.

5. If you had a <u>benefactor</u>, what would you like him or her to do for you?

6. Look through your local newspaper for one day and make a list of the crimes various <u>malefactors</u> have committed.

Power Words

1. **hone**   hōn   verb

   To make perfect or complete

   Lindsay had **honed** her teaching skills *to perfection* since she had been teaching for 30 years.

   To sharpen with a stone

   The neighbors wondered why Justin was **honing** his knife until they saw the *rabbit that he had trapped* in the forest.

   Synonyms: prepare, sharpen

2. **nuance**   nyōō'äns'   noun

   A subtle or slight degree of difference, as in meaning, feeling, or tone

   The teacher told her class to observe the **nuances** *between the author's early writings and his later ones.*

   Synonyms: shading, difference

3. **bevy**   bĕv'ē   noun

   A group or an assemblage of a group

   Every year the pageant promoters gather a **bevy** *of beautiful women* to compete for the title of Miss America.

   Synonyms: swarm, collection, cluster

Practice Exercises

1. What skill do you have that you would like to <u>hone</u>? How would you go about doing that?

2. Explain the <u>nuances</u> between *collaborate* and *cooperate*.

3. List three things that could be classified as a <u>bevy</u>.

Chapter Review

Yes or No?

Read the sentence and answer the question.

1. Because she was cold, Lisa got out her <u>thermal</u> blanket and turned up the <u>thermostat</u> to get warm.

   a. Would the blanket keep her warm? _____

   b. Did she have a way to make her house warmer? _____

2. When they were assigned to co-manage the new project, Joe and Jenny were very <u>flexible</u> and tried to be <u>compatible</u> with each other.

   a. Did Joe and Jenny argue a lot? _____

   b. Were they each stubborn and did they stick with their own ideas? _____

3. The audience thought the magician was <u>telepathic</u>, but really his assistant was <u>telecommunicating</u> with him through a wire taped to his ear.

   a. Did the audience think the magician was able to communicate without words? _____

   b. Was the magician talking to his assistant on a telephone? _____

4. The <u>benefactors</u> named the music program in the school as a <u>beneficiary</u> in their will.

   a. Did they want to do good things for the music program?_____

   b. Did the music program get money from the will? _____

Expanded Word Forms

autonomy	autonomous	malign	maligning	maligned
compatible	compatibility	compatibly	flexible	flexibility

1. Jack and Jill were very _____. Their friends all envied their _____.
   When they went up the hill and fell down again, they did it very _____.

2. The gymnastics champion was very _____. Her _____ enabled her to earn higher scores on the balance beam portion of her program.

3. When you are 18 you are thought to be _____ and able to make your own decisions. That _____ feels great, but sometimes you still need to ask for help.

4. Do not say nasty things and _____ your friends. By _____ them, you will hurt their feelings. If someone is _____, he or she will not be happy.

Expand Your Learning

You learned in Chapter One that it is important to use a variety of strategies when learning and reviewing material. Do one or more of the following exercises to practice the words in this chapter.

Using your vision and color:

1. Write the words on note cards. Put the word on the front and the definition on the back. Use a different-color ink for the different categories of words according to the various word parts. To review the words, you should use three steps.

a. Pronounce the word on the front.
b. Try to remember the definition in your own words.
c. Look at the back to check your answer.

Separate the words into two piles, the ones you know and the ones you missed. Keep reviewing the ones you missed until you can recite them all correctly. You should repeat this several times during the week. Be sure to mix up the cards so you do not always do them in the same order.

2. Group the words according to their different word parts. Write each group in a different-color ink. Outline the shape of each word.

3. Draw simple stick figures to illustrate the meaning of each word.

4. Go back to the Fill in the Blank exercises and underline the context clues in each sentence that helped you identify the correct word.

5. Find other words that use the word parts in this chapter. Keep a list of words with each word part and add to it as you find more words throughout the semester.

Using your voice and hearing:

1. Make note cards as explained in the preceding exercise using vision. You do not need to use different-color inks unless you want to. When you go through the cards, say the words and the definitions out loud.

2. Go back to the Fill in the Blank exercises and read the sentences out loud. This would be a good way for you to check that you have used each word correctly.

Using large and small muscles:

1. Fold a piece of paper in half lengthwise and label the columns A and B. Write the words in column A and the definitions in B. Fold back column A and recite the words from the definitions, then do the reverse. Review the words as you do some sort of physical activity such as walking or riding an exercise bike.

2. Put the words and definitions on note cards as explained in the preceding exercise using vision. You do not need to use different-color inks unless you want to. Carry these cards with you and review them throughout the day as you do your daily activities such as brushing your teeth, eating breakfast, etc.

Answers to Confusing Words

threw, through
there, their
due, do
then, than

Puzzle Fun

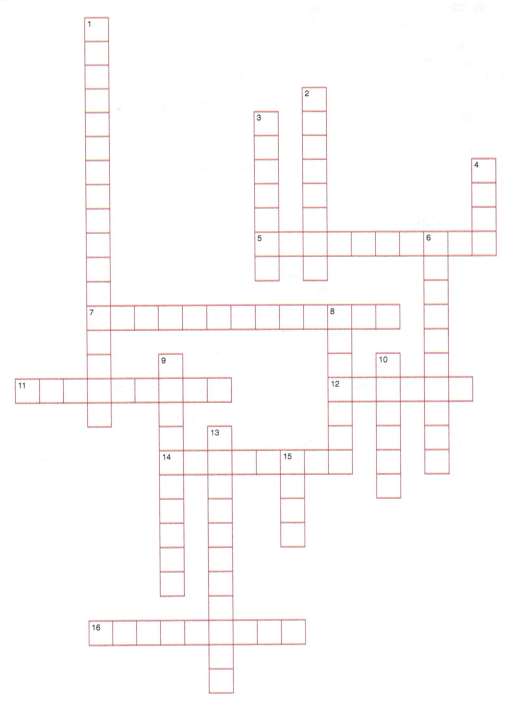

Across

5. if you are unsuited for each other you are not this
7. journals and memoirs are usually written as this
11. movie stars are always asked for this—their signature
12. a subtle difference
14. characteristics of this word are pliable and adaptable
16. *clairvoyance* is a synonym for this word

Down

1. communicating from a distance
2. *freedom* and *liberty* are synonyms
3. children use this to help them learn to read
4. to make perfect or complete
6. another word for this is *supporter*
8. the smallest phonetic unit in a language that is capable of conveying a distinction in meaning
9. a criminal
10. the opposite of this word is *kindness*
13. a receiver of the good
15. synonyms for this word might be *collection* and *cluster*

CHAPTER TEN
Language Is Always Changing

Man's command of the language is most important. Next to kissing,
it's the most exciting form of communication.

Oren Arnold, novelist (1900–1980)

CHAPTER OBJECTIVE

Students will be able to identify and use words with the following common structural elements:

Prefixes: semi-, sub-, man-, manu-
Suffixes: -ee, -ate, -ize

CHAPTER OUTLINE

 Memory Tip   Learning Never Ends

 Vocabulary Strategy   Language Is Always Changing

Part A
Words to Learn

refugee
referee
substandard
submerge
subterranean
semiconscious
semiannual

Structural Elements

semi-
sub-
-ee

Part B
Words to Learn

manual
manipulate
manuscript
dramatize
utilize
normalize
validate

Structural Elements

man, manu-
-ize
-ate

Power Words

enumerate
justify

Memory Tip   Learning Never Ends

You are nearing the end of this vocabulary book, but learning never has an end. You will continue to come across new words in your everyday listening and reading. Remember to use structural elements and context clues to figure out the meanings of these words. And once you have run into a word more than once, it is time to apply the strategies covered in this book to learn the new word.

As you study for your career there will be many words specific to that field or discipline. In fact, some of these words may only be used in the context of the discipline. In other cases the discipline-specific definitions may not apply when the words are used in everyday language. In your textbooks you will find many context clues when a word is first introduced. Again, use the strategies presented here to learn these words as soon as you run into them.

And finally enjoy language and the learning of new words!

Vocabulary Strategy   Language Is Always Changing

Our English language is always changing. Words suddenly become popular and start appearing frequently in what we are reading. Some examples of words that are currently appearing frequently are:

- *ubiquitous* (adjective), being everywhere

- *egregious* (adjective), very bad

- *hubris* (noun), excessive pride

The meaning of words also can change over time. Here are some examples of words that have developed new and different meanings:

- *cool*—either a low temperature or something good and current

- *web*—either something created by a spider or the Internet

- *lame*—either having a disabled leg or arm or something that is weak or not good

- *swipe*—either to steal or what you do with your credit card in a machine

What other examples can you and your classmates think of?

Part A

WORDS TO LEARN—SEE AND SAY   Use the pronunciation guide on the first page of this book to help you SAY each word.

1. refugee	rĕf′yo͞o-jē′
2. referee	rĕf′ə-rē′
3. substandard	sŭb-stăn′dərd
4. submerge	səb-mûrj′
5. subterranean	sŭb′tə-rā′nē-ən
6. semiconscious	sĕm′ē-kŏn′shəs
7. semiannual	sĕm′ē-ăn′yo͞o-əl

STRUCTURAL ELEMENTS   Look at the structural elements of each word. Use these elements to unlock the word's meaning.

semi-	half
sub-	under, below
-ee	one who

CONTEXT CLUES   Read the sentences. Use the words around the unfamiliar word to determine the word's meaning. Words in bold are the vocabulary words; words in italic are context clues.

1. **Refugees** from across the area *fled over the border to reach the safety* of the neighboring country.

2. Because they could not agree, Max and Mathilda asked their lawyer to **referee** their dispute about selling their house during the divorce and *help them come to an agreement.*

3. The house was in *shambles and falling down* because of the **substandard** construction material.

4. In order to get the skunk smell off his dog, Mark had to completely **submerge** the dog in a *bath of tomato juice.*

5. In the science fiction movie, the hero rode a **subterranean** vehicle *below the earth's surface.*

6. Joyce *woke up in the middle of the night*, and in her **semiconscious** state she stubbed her toe on the chair in her bedroom.

7. I see my dentist **semiannually**, *in the spring and again in the fall.*

 DICTIONARY   Read the following definitions.

1. **refugee**   rĕf'yoo-jē'   noun

   Etymology: re (back) fuge (to flee) ee (one who)

   Someone who leaves his or her country, especially during a war or other threatening event

   Thousands of **refugees** have entered the camps along the borders *to escape the tragic conditions in their country.*

   Synonym: evacuee

2. **referee**   rĕf'ə-rē'   noun

   Etymology: refer (to direct or send) ee (one who)

   One to whom something is referred, especially for a settlement, a decision, or an opinion as to the thing's quality

   The **referee** at the hearing was *fair in his decision* to make both parties pay equally since he found them equally at fault for the accident.

   Vocabulary Tip: *Referee* originally referred to a person appointed by the British Parliament to examine patent applications (1621) and was formed from English *refer* and *–ee*. The sense of "an arbitrator or person to whom a dispute is referred" was first recorded in 1690; by 1840 the word acquired the further sense of "the judge of play in games and sports." Baseball, boxing, and cricket have *umpires*; basketball, hockey, rugby, and football have *referees*—and American football has both. (thesaurus.com)

3. **substandard**   sŭb-stăn'dərd   adjective

   Etymology: sub (below) standard (model or guide)

   Failing to meet a standard, below standard

   The school district had to decide whether it would close two of the *low-performing* schools in the district because they consistently were getting **substandard** scores at all grade levels.

   Synonym: inferior

   Antonym: superior

4. **submerge**   səb-mûrj'   verb

   Etymology: sub (under) merge (to plunge or immerse)

   To cover or hide something completely

While taking college classes it is important to **submerge** yourself *in the material* so that you completely understand it.

To put something completely underwater

The swimming coach told her class to **submerge** their heads *underwater* for ten seconds to begin to develop endurance.

Synonym: drench

5. **subterranean**   sŭb'tə-rā'nē-ən   adjective

Etymology: sub (under) terra (earth or ground) ean (relates to)

Under the ground

Many companies are now aggressively exploring **subterranean** sources of energy since equipment to go *below the earth's surface* has advanced tremendously through the years.

6. **semiconscious**   sĕm'ē-kŏn'shəs   adjective

Etymology: semi (half) conscious (aware)

Partially conscious; not completely aware of sensations

After the car accident, Darren was only **semiconscious** so the paramedics took him to the hospital to be observed *until he was completely awake and alert.*

7. **semiannual**   sĕm'ē-ăn'yōō-əl   adjective

Etymology: semi (half) annu (year) al (relates to or pertains to)

Occurring or issued twice a year

The **semiannual** furniture sale is usually *in February and August.*

Vocabulary Tip: *Semiannual* refers to an occurrence two times a year; *biannual* refers to an occurrence every two years. (See structural element *bi-* in Chapter 5, Part A.)

Practice Exercises

MULTIPLE CHOICE

1. Which of the following is a responsibility of a <u>referee</u>?
   a. to help the home team win
   b. to give each side of a competition or debate an equal chance
   c. to help the antiestablishment candidate overthrow the government
   d. to provide an antidote

2. Which of the following describes a <u>refugee</u>?
   a. shopping for new clothes
   b. looking for the closest Starbucks
   c. looking for an antidote for a snake bite
   d. looking for a safe place to live

3. Which of the following would describe <u>substandard</u> school work?
   a. accurate, neat
   b. sloppy, careless
   c. on time, followed directions
   d. well-developed ideas

4. Which of the following would you <u>submerge</u>?
   a. dirty dishes in your sink
   b. pizza delivered to your door
   c. your desire to earn a degree
   d. your vacuum cleaner

5. Which of the following could be described as being <u>subterranean</u>?
   a. moles
   b. birds
   c. worms
   d. both a and c
   e. all of the above

6. Which of the following describes someone who is <u>semiconscious</u>?
   a. sleeping peacefully
   b. fully involved in the conversation
   c. actively listening
   d. partly alert

7. If you have a <u>semiannual</u> appointment with your dentist, how often do you see her?
   a. once a year
   b. every six months
   c. when you have a toothache
   d. every two years

FILL IN THE BLANK   Select the BEST word for each sentence. Use each word only once.

refugee	referee	substandard	submerged
subterranean	semiconscious	semiannually	

1. After the accident Mike was _____ and did not know where he was.

2. When team A broke the rules, the _____ stopped the game and administered a penalty.

3. During her college career, Meagan met with her advisor _____, once in the spring and once in the fall, to plan her courses for the next semester.

4. The government established several _____ camps to house the people seeking safety in their country.

5. The _____ stream ran right below the surface of the ground.

6. I had to ask the man from the nursery to replace all of the new plants. They died right away because of their _____ quality.

7. After the accident Joe scrambled to safety and climbed onto dry land as his car _____ in the lake.

CORRECT OR INCORRECT?   If the sentence is correct, write a "C" on the line provided. If not, write an "I" for incorrect, then REWRITE the sentence to make it correct. You can change any part of the sentence to make it correct.

1. The <u>refugee</u> family was helped by several local people to establish a new home in our community.

   _____

2. <u>Referees</u> are used in football games and boxing matches to be sure that all of the rules are followed.

   _____

3. I appreciate high-quality material and was very happy with the <u>substandard</u> material in my new coat.

   _____

4. My cat hates to get wet, so she played happily when she was <u>submerged</u> in the bathtub.

   _____

5. The <u>subterranean</u> bird flew through the air and built nests in trees.

   _____

6. During the lecture John was so interested in the topic and so involved taking notes that his friends thought he was <u>semiconscious</u>.

   _____

7. I drive many miles each week, so I get my car's oil changed <u>semiannually</u>, at least every other month.

   _____

SHORT ANSWER   Write your answers on a separate sheet of paper.

1. Name three things that a <u>refugee</u> might flee.

2. Describe an experience when you would have liked someone to <u>referee</u> the events.

3. Make a two-column chart. In one column list five characteristics of <u>substandard</u> work. In the other column list words that mean the opposite and would describe excellent work. The type of work can be from any area: academics, construction, cooking, etc.

4. List three things that can be <u>submerged</u>.

5. Draw a picture showing a cross section of ground and draw two <u>subterranean</u> animals and two non-<u>subterranean</u> animals in their correct locations.

6. What are three words that would describe someone who is <u>semiconscious</u>? Three words to describe someone fully conscious?

7. What are two things you do or would want to happen <u>semiannually</u>? What about annually?

Part B

WORDS TO LEARN—SEE AND SAY   Use the pronunciation guide on the first page of this book to help you SAY each word.

1.	manual	măn′yōō-əl
2.	manipulate	mə-nĭp′yə-lāt′
3.	manuscript	măn′yə-skrĭpt′
4.	dramatize	drăm′ə-tīz′
5.	utilize	yōōt′l-īz′
6.	normalize	nôr′mə-līz′
7.	validate	văl′ĭ-dāt′

 STRUCTURAL ELEMENTS   Look at the structural elements of each word. Use these elements to unlock the word's meaning.

man, manu-	hand
-ize	to make or cause to be
-ate	to make or cause to be

CONTEXT CLUES   Read the sentences. Use the words around the unfamiliar word to determine the word's meaning. Words in bold are the vocabulary words; words in italic are context clues.

1. Seth didn't have any power tools, so he had to hammer and screw in the nails **manually**, *by hand.*

2. Whenever Marie gets a new appliance, the first thing she does is *read* the **manual.** She want to know *how everything works* before starting to use it.

3. The immoral bookkeeper **manipulated**, *or changed*, the numbers so that no one would know she was stealing from the company.

4. J.K. Rowlings *wrote* many of the *Harry Potter* **manuscripts** while sitting at her local coffee shop.

5. The first-grade class *put on a play* and **dramatized** their favorite story for their parents at the open house.

6. When studying, it is a good idea to *take advantage of* and **utilize** all of the tutoring services offered by your school.

7. When the district decided to **normalize** the food served by the cafeterias in all three schools and *make all the menus the same*, the students missed the specialties of their individual cooks.

8. John had to **validate**, *or prove*, that his parents saw his report card, so he asked them to sign their names at the bottom.

 DICTIONARY   Read the following definitions.

1. **manual**   măn′yōō-əl   adjective/noun

   Etymology: manu (hand) al (relates or pertains to)

   (adjective) Done by hand

   Before Eli Whitney invented the cotton gin, picking cotton was a **manual** job, *done by hand.*

   (noun) A small reference book, especially one giving instructions

   Jeff lost the *owner's* **manual** for his new car, *so he could not figure out how to change the clock for daylight saving time.*

   Synonym: (noun) handbook, guide

2. **manipulate**   mə-nĭp′yə-lāt′   verb

   Etymology: man(u) (hand) ate (to make)

   To influence, manage, or control to one's advantage by artful or indirect means

   The secretary tried to **manipulate** her boss *to give her a raise* since she knew he liked her and her work.

   To handle something skillfully; to move, arrange, operate, or control by the hands or by mechanical means

   The second-grade teacher had *colored blocks* that the students could **manipulate** and *move around* to help them understand addition and subtraction.

   Synonym: maneuver

3. **manuscript**   măn′yə-skrĭpt′   noun

   Etymology: manu (hand) script (something written)

   A book, document, or other composition written by hand

   The original **manuscript**, *handwritten by the author*, would be worth thousands of dollars but the copied book was worth less than a hundred dollars.

4. **dramatize** drăm′ə-tīz′ verb

   Etymology: drama (composition for theatrical presentation) ize (to make or cause to be)

   To adapt a literary work or other event for dramatic presentation

   Anytime you see a movie or TV show about real events, the *actors* are **dramatizing** *what really happened.*

   Synonym: perform

5. **utilize** yōōt′l-īz′ verb

   Etymology: uti (useful) ize (to make or cause to be)

   To put to use, especially to find a profitable or practical use

   Let's make sure we **utilize** our resources as *effectively* as possible.

   Vocabulary Tip: *Utilize* means to "use in a practical and effective way" and is more specific than *use*, which is a more general word.

   Synonym: employ

6. **normalize** nôr′mə-līz′ verb

   Etymology: normal (regular or standare) ize (to make or cause to be)

   To make normal, especially to cause to conform to a standard or norm

   After Hurricane Katrina it was hard for the citizens of New Orleans to try to **normalize** their daily lives and *return to their normal routines.*

7. **validate** văl′ĭ-dāt′ verb

   Etymology: valid (proper or legal) ate (to make or cause to be)

   To declare or make legally valid; to officially prove that something is true or correct

   The therapist **validated** Sue's feelings and told her that *however she was feeling was right for her.*

   Synonym: authenticate, verify

   Antonym: disprove

Practice Exercises

MULTIPLE CHOICE

1. Which of the following is a definition for <u>manual</u>?
   a. by hand
   b. using the latest technology
   c. an instruction book
   d. both a and c
   e. all of the above

2. Which of the following is something you can <u>manipulate</u>?
   a. a poem you are memorizing
   b. the smell of freshly cut grass
   c. jigsaw puzzle pieces
   d. the melody of your favorite song

3. Which of the following would involve a <u>manuscript</u>?
   a. a new popular song
   b. a novel
   c. rules for baseball
   d. a laptop computer

4. Which of the following shows someone <u>dramatizing</u> an event?
   a. a football player dancing in the end zone after a touchdown
   b. a group discussion to solve a problem
   c. a sleeping baby
   d. the complex pattern of air traffic at an airport

5. Which of the following might you <u>utilize</u> when you are cleaning your house or apartment?
   a. a mop or broom
   b. a plan about how to spend your time
   c. garbage bags
   d. all of the above
   e. none of the above

6. What would instructors do if they wanted to <u>normalize</u> the final exam in several sections of the same course?
   a. Make sure each class took a different exam.
   b. Make some exams multiple choice and some essay.
   c. Have some classes write papers and others take an exam.
   d. Give every student the same exam.

7. What happens if a company <u>validates</u> your parking ticket for the parking garage?
   a. It doubles the parking fee.
   b. It pays the parking free for you and mark your ticket paid.
   c. It replaces your lost ticket.
   d. It has your car towed.

FILL IN THE BLANK   Select the BEST answer for each sentence. Use each word only once.

| manually | manipulate | manuscript | dramatized |
| utilized | normalize | validated | |

1. Josh wrote the _____ of his novel that he submitted to the publisher by hand.

2. For their final class project in the Introduction to Dance class, Mary's group performed a dance that _____ a college football game.

3. John was an expert auto mechanic because he worked well with his hands and like to do things _____.

4. June liked to sew and quilt because she liked to _____ the different colors and pieces to make a new pattern.

5. Jenny _____ the Tutoring Center for help with her Spanish I class.

6. Dr. James _____ Sue's feelings by stating that many of her patients felt the same way.

7. In order to _____ the testing experience for each group taking the test, the person in charge read each group the same directions.

CORRECT OR INCORRECT?   If the sentence is correct, write a "C" on the line provided. If not, write an "I" for incorrect, then REWRITE the sentence to make it correct. You can change any part of the sentence to make it correct.

1. Miss Smith had many <u>manual</u> objects to help her first-grade students understand math. They learned best when they could <u>manipulate</u> objects to practice adding and subtracting.

_____

2. Vince liked to study using his vision and hearing. He learned best when he could <u>manipulate</u> the information.

_____

3. Ellie sent the completed <u>manuscript</u> to the publisher a week before the deadline.

_____

4. The <u>dramatization</u> of the intervention that resulted in the main character going into rehab was very moving.

_____

5. Dale <u>utilized</u> the argument between his two friends in order to help them solve their dispute.

_____

6. Miss Parker <u>normalized</u> the activities at the day care center so that each child had a unique experience and could pick what he or she wanted to do each day.

_____

7. The witness <u>validated</u> the convict's story when he proved it was false.

_____

SHORT ANSWER   Write your answers on a separate sheet of paper.

1. When you learn, what strategies can you use where you are <u>manually</u> working with the information?

2. Think about your normal day. What are three things that you <u>manipulate</u>?

3. Name two things you use during the week that would have started with a <u>manuscript</u>.

4. Describe how a child would act if he <u>dramatized</u> a small cut he received on the playground.

5. Name three strategies that you <u>utilize</u> when you are studying.

6. Name one activity or experience you have had that has been <u>normalized</u> for everyone and one activity that has been individualized.

7. Name two times when you had something <u>validated</u>.

Power Words

1. **enumerate**   ĭ-nōō′mə-rāt′   verb

   To count off or name one by one; list; to determine the number of

   The president's spokesperson **enumerated** the steps *one by one* that would be taken to improve health care.

   Synonyms: list, count, itemize

2. **justify**   jŭs′tə-fī′   verb

   To demonstrate or prove to be just, right, or valid

   Mallory's teacher asked her to **justify** her answers and *reasoning.*

   Synonyms: confirm, verify

Practice Exercises

1. <u>Enumerate</u> the top five qualities you would like in a friend,

2. How would each of the following <u>justify</u> his or her request?
   a. a teenager who wants to stay out past his or her curfew
   b. a child who wants his or her parent to stop smoking
   c. a toddler who wants candy in the grocery store

Chapter Review

Yes or No?

Read the sentence and answer the questions.

1. The <u>refugees</u> were escaping <u>substandard</u> living conditions.

   a. Were the people staying in their home country? _____

   b. Were they enjoying pleasant living? _____

2. Members of the Polar Bear Club <u>submerge</u> themselves in freezing water on New Year's Day.

   a. Do they get completely wet? _____

3. In order to <u>utilize</u> the new cell phone, Jeff had to read the <u>manual</u> and learn how to <u>manipulate</u> the device.

   a. Did Jeff want to give away his new phone? _____

   b. Was there material to help him learn how the phone works? _____

   c. Did Jeff use his hands to work the phone? _____

4. The trainer hoped to <u>normalize</u> the wild dog's behavior in order to <u>justify</u> bringing the dog home to live with his family.

   a. Did the trainer encourage the dog's wild behavior? _____

   b. Was the trainer looking for a reason to keep the dog? _____

Expanded Word Forms

submerged	dramatized	dramatizing	dramatizations
enumerated	enumerating	enumeration	submerge	submerging
validation	validate		

1. Sybil _____ all the reasons why her family should move to a new house. By _____ the reasons she was able to convince her husband to see her point of view. The _____ also helped them understand what they would need in a new house.

2. When washing dishes, you _____ the dishes in hot, soapy water. While _____ the dishes you also have to do the same with your hands. When everything is _____ you can begin to wash and clean the dishes.

3. The teenagers _____ every event that happened during the day. Their _____ finally got on their parents' nerves and the parents told them to stop _____ everything.

4. When he was at his doctor's office Mark asked the receptionist to _____ his parking ticket. The _____ stamp meant that he did not have to pay for parking that day.

Expand Your Learning

You learned in Chapter One that it is important to use a variety of strategies when learning and reviewing material. Do one or more of the following exercises to practice the words in this chapter.

Using your vision and color:

1. Write the words on note cards. Put the word on the front and the definition on the back. Use a different-color ink for the different categories of words according to the various word parts. To review the words, you should use three steps.
   a. Pronounce the word on the front.
   b. Try to remember the definition in your own words.
   c. Look at the back to check your answer.

   Separate the words into two piles, the ones you know and the ones you missed. Keep reviewing the ones you missed until you can recite them all correctly. You should repeat this several times during the week. Be sure to mix up the cards so you do not always do them in the same order.

2. Group the words according to their different word parts. Write each group in a different-color ink. Outline the shape of each word.

3. Draw simple stick figures to illustrate the meaning of each word.

4. Go back to the Fill in the Blank exercises and underline the context clues in each sentence that helped you identify the correct word.

5. Find other words that use the word parts in this chapter. Keep a list of words with each word part and add to it as you find more words throughout the semester.

Using your voice and hearing:

1. Make note cards as explained in the preceding exercise using vision. You do not need to use different-color inks unless you want to. When you go through the cards, say the words and the definitions out loud.

2. Go back to the Fill in the Blank exercises and read the sentences out loud. This would be a good way for you to check that you have used each word correctly.

Using large and small muscles:

1. Fold a piece of paper in half lengthwise and label the columns A and B. Write the words in column A and the definitions in B. Fold back column A and recite the words from the definitions, then do the reverse. Review the words as you do some sort of physical activity such as walking or riding an exercise bike.

2. Put the words and definitions on note cards as explained in the preceding exercise using vision. You do not need to use different-color inks unless you want to. Carry these cards with you and review them throughout the day as you do your daily activities such as brushing your teeth, eating breakfast, etc.

Puzzle Fun

Read each hint. Select the synonym, antonym, or definition for each word.

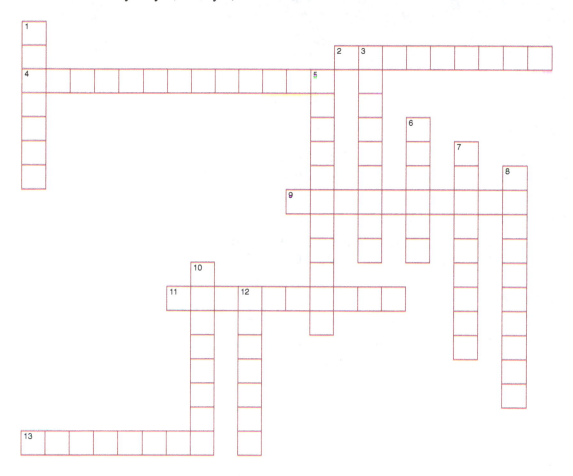

Across

2. *count* and *itemize* are synonyms for this word
4. not completely aware of sensations
9. *maneuver* is a synonym for this word
11. a document or other composition written by hand
13. *drench* is a synonym for this word

Down

1. *verify* is a synonym for this word
3. to conform to a standard
5. *superior* is an antonym for this word
6. done by hand
7. *perform* is a synonym for this word
8. occurring twice a year
10. to officially prove that something is true or correct
12. to put to use

APPENDIX A

ANSWERS TO MULTIPLE CHOICE QUESTIONS

Chapter Two

| **Part A:** | 1. a | 2. c | 3. a | 4. d | 5. c | 6. a | 7. d | 8. d |
| **Part B:** | 1. a | 2. a | 3. c | 4. c | 5. a | 6. c | 7. c | |

Chapter Three

| **Part A:** | 1. b | 2. c | 3. a | 4. c | 5. c | 6. e | 7. d |
| **Part B:** | 1. b | 2. a | 3. d | 4. c | 5. d | 6. b | 7. d |

Chapter Four

| **Part A:** | 1. d | 2. a | 3. c | 4. a | 5. a | 6. d | 7. b | 8. a |
| **Part B:** | 1. a | 2. b | 3. c | 4. b | 5. b | 6. a | 7. d | |

Chapter Five

| **Part A:** | 1. a | 2. a | 3. c | 4. b | 5. c | 6. b | 7. d |
| **Part B:** | 1. d | 2. d | 3. a | 4. a | 5. b | 6. c | 7. d |

Chapter Six

| **Part A:** | 1. a | 2. c | 3. d | 4. a | 5. b | 6. d | 7. c | |
| **Part B:** | 1. c | 2. a | 3. d | 4. a | 5. c | 6. b | 7. e | 8. a |

Chapter Seven

| **Part A:** | 1. b | 2. b | 3. c | 4. b | 5. b | 6. d | 7. c | |
| **Part B:** | 1. a | 2. d | 3. c | 4. b | 5. a | 6. c | 7. a | 8. d |

Chapter Eight

| **Part A:** | 1. d | 2. a | 3. c | 4. a | 5. b | 6. d | 7. b |
| **Part B:** | 1. d | 2. a | 3. b | 4. c | 5. a | 6. b | 7. c |

Chapter Nine

| **Part A:** | 1. c | 2. b | 3. b | 4. b | 5. b | 6. d | 7. d | |
| **Part B:** | 1. d | 2. e | 3. c | 4. e | 5. e | 6. b | 7. b | 8. c |

NOTE: Part B, #5—a benefactor can give various types of aid; it does not have to be money.

Chapter Ten

| **Part A:** | 1. b | 2. d | 3. b | 4. a | 5. d | 6. d | 7. b |
| **Part B:** | 1. d | 2. c | 3. b | 4. a | 5. d | 6. d | 7. b |

APPENDIX B

WORD LIST WITH CHAPTER NUMBERS

Word	Chapter	Word	Chapter
abdicate	5	dilemma	5
abide	5	dramatize	10
adage	5	eccentric	7
aerobic	3	embrace	7
affiliation	2	emit	7
alternative	7	empathy	7
analyze	8	enable	7
antidote	2	engage	7
antiestablishment	2	entrench	7
antiseptic	2	enumerate	10
antisocial	2	exceed	7
appropriate	3	excerpt	2
archaeologist	5	excessive	7
archaeology	5	exhale	7
autobiography	9	exotic	3
autograph	9	facial	3
autonomy	9	facsimile	6
benefactor	9	flexible	9
beneficiary	9	geocentric	6
bevy	9	geography	6
bilateral	5	geology	6
chronic	8	gerontologist	5
chronological	8	gerontology	5
coherent	8	graphic	4
collaborate	8	graphology	4
colleagues	8	hone	9
compatible	9	illegal	4
compromise	8	illogical	4
constituent	8	immoral	4
convince	8	improper	4
cooperation	8	inconsistent	4
critical	3	inference	2
deactivate	4	infuriate	4
decline	4	inhale	4
deplete	4	interim	6
detract	4	interpersonal	6

Word	Chapter	Word	Chapter
interstate	6	quadruple	5
intramural	6	react	3
intrastate	6	reduce	3
irregular	4	referee	10
irrelevant	4	refugee	10
justify	10	reinforce	3
logical	3	relate	3
macrocosm	8	residential	3
macroeconomics	8	retaliation	3
malefactor	9	retroactive	5
malice	9	retrospect	5
manipulate	10	revelation	3
manual	10	revolution	3
manuscript	10	semiannual	10
microeconomics	8	semiconscious	10
microorganism	8	spawn	8
microscope	8	submerge	10
monopoly	5	substandard	10
morgue	6	subterranean	10
mortal	6	surpass	4
mortician	6	synthesize	8
mortify	6	telecommunication	9
nondescript	7	telegraph	4
nonsense	7	telepathy	9
normalize	10	thematic	3
nuance	9	theologian	5
objective	7	theology	5
opaque	7	thermal	9
optimist	3	thermostat	9
organic	3	transfer	2
passive	7	transition	2
pentagon	5	translucent	7
pessimist	3	transmit	2
phoneme	9	transparent	7
phonics	9	transport	2
poise	4	trilogy	5
postpone	2	unilateral	5
postscript	2	utilize	10
precede	2	valid	6
predict	2	validate	10
preface	2	verbose	6
prefix	2	vicarious	6
preview	2	vitality	6
proactive	5	vivacious	6
provoke	5		